Christians and Their Money

Christians and Their Money

What the Bible says about Finances

Richard Baland and A. H. Barbee

To order additional copies, please contact us.
BookSurge, LLC
www.booksurge.com
1-866-308-6235
orders@booksurge.com

Christians and Their Money

Table of Contents

INTRODUCTION

Christians and Their Money is not your typical book. It is more accurately described as a series of questions and answers. Throughout this book we insist on each believers' responsibility to practice due diligence. While the message we explore definitely deals with material possessions, it is embedded in spiritual truth. Christians and Their Money is saturated with Scripture to teach about what is right and possibly wrong with how, why, from whom and to whom believers gain and give money.

We identify dangers faced by anyone who is or wants to be wealthy, especially members of the household of faith. We cite the difficulty for spiritual leaders who minister at-a-distance to stay off the slippery slope that leads to using religion as the road to riches.

We also provide ways to help contributors determine what ministers and ministries they should or should not support. We recommend questions sincere donors may ask themselves and any ministry to which they might contribute. Believers should confront the suspect and commend the genuine. Gifts to the wrong ministry costs money and blessings. Yet, Christians need not suffer losses for lack of information. God's Word is filled with directions about how to have and how to handle money—this includes the truth about who deserves support and how much should be given.

Christians and Their Money explores weak spots in the beliefs and behavior of many in God's family, with regard to material matters. We show, in this book, how even ministers, who may otherwise be faithful to the Word, encourage their followers to violate Biblical teaching about giving.

Some will find the message about having and handling money in Christians and Their Money disturbing. Others will discover Biblical teachings and see the message about money, ministers and ministries with blinders removed—their eyes will open to truth that sets them free.

In Christians and Their Money, we urge believers to embrace Biblically sanctioned practices to handle income in ways that honor the Lord, and how to be released from the bondage of debt. We want to enable members of God's family to discern what His work is and encourage support that pleases the Lord.

Christians and Their Money offers spiritual and practical direction for believers who are sincere about identifying the Biblical priorities for earning, spending, saving, investing and giving. Our step-by-step plan of action for serious believers may be adopted to help them succeed at any stage in their financial life.

CHAPTER 1

LET'S TALK ABOUT MONEY

Any one may so arrange his affairs that his taxes shall be as low as possible; he is not bound to choose that pattern which will best pay the treasury; there is not even a patriotic duty to increase one's taxes." Judge Learned Hand

Money is one of the most sensitive subjects to discuss among Christians. Over the years, when counseling pastors, missionaries and other spiritual leaders we have found most are hesitant to speak openly about this subject. Many think they will be branded as someone in ministry who is "just after your money."

Too often the issue of compensation creates conflict in pastor/people relations. Frequently faith missionaries—those not related to a denomination—who must derive support directly from individuals and churches, fear telling people their actual needs. Almost anyone in ministry knows about churches and Christian organizations where God's servants are pressured with false guilt for raising questions about what or how they are paid.

Negative Attitude

The negative attitude directed toward Christian workers is not biblical. It stands against truth. Paul taught Timothy that true spiritual leaders deserve to be paid. He even used this argument when defending himself against unfair accusations some in the Church at Corinth flung at him. Although he generally chose not to seek payment for himself, Paul was adamant about people in the Lord's work being properly paid.

Would we send someone to war expecting them to pay their own way? Would someone work in the field or milk cows and not get anything to eat or drink? Or, would anybody raise cattle but not give them anything to eat?

After clearly stressing his right to be paid, Paul explained that he served sacrificially. It is important to understand that this was his voluntary choice. He did not teach that anyone else had to make the same decision regarding service. If others chose to follow Paul's model of sacrifice in ministry and essentially being self-supporting, their choice, like his, must be voluntary.

Therefore, for sacrifice to be of the quality that honors God, it can only be and must only be voluntary. Forced sacrifice is a demonstration of dishonor—dishonor on the part of those who force others to sacrifice and dishonor to the Word of God that teaches about paying spiritual leaders.

Paul set two examples in his discussion with the Corinthians about his right to receive payment for spiritual service. First, he showed all other spiritual leaders that they could and should speak about practical material matters freely; Second, Paul explained that true sacrifice in ministry must be a voluntary decision, not forced.

Money and Marriage

Not only do many ministers have difficulty talking about money, so does the typical married couple. Although disagreements over money is a key factor that contributes to marital problems among the population in general, facing facts about having and handling money is still placed on the back burner in most households.

How does marriage relate to managing money? Is there a Biblical order for the following important issues we face: marriage, children, investment, career, college, apprenticeship, engagement, and house hunting? Let's see.

People today fall in love, get married, buy a house and then go to college or look for a job. That is backwards. The order should be college, job, house, and then marriage. Young couples want what Mom and Dad have. They often overlook that Mom and Dad worked and saved for at least 40 years to reach their income and living level.

We note a practical pattern for young men to follow. It is the ongoing practice among Jewish males, which has a Biblical base.

By age thirteen, boys should have an indication of your interests, skills, talents, gifts, aptitude and abilities. Why thirteen? This is the recognized age when a Jewish boy becomes a man. This means more than assuming a role in the synagogue. It means, throughout much of Jewish history, he assumed a significant role in the family business.

Scriptures teach this principle. By age 13 each son in a Christian home should have received sufficient experience to know which direction they will go. If gifted academically, they would be in honors or gifted and talented classes by this age. Dad should help each son to determine their direction. Every year invested on the wrong path is a year lost in the son's future career.

For centuries the Hebrew man had a business or career and a house before his parents arranged his marriage. The objective is clear. While our society does not want parents to select our mates for marriage, the basic pattern is practical—build your business before your marriage.

Essentially, in Jewish history, fathers trained their sons from age five to age 13, in contrast to Christian fathers who entrust this training to their wives—the mother of their children. Since Orthodox Jewish families are one wage earner, that being the father, since he as trainer and wage earner are the same, the sons learn from the greater interest on finances. This too is different from the typical Christian household. So we have something to learn from Jewish families—the Biblical lesson already noted of training up a child in the way he should go.

Similarly, in both Old Testament and New Testament

teaching, instruction for both spiritual and practical development is found in the relationship between older and younger women. Older women are to teach younger women.

But the weightier principle was in ancient times placed on the males. And that principle, which is the third priority in our plan of action for believers, informs males to establish a training plan for earning a living before they marry. This scheme may include college, technical school or association with a craftsperson, but it will be set and should be fulfilled before marriage. So we put it like this: build your business (which may mean your career) before you build your house—"house" referring to both your marriage and family and the actual house you may build and in which you may live.

Can you imagine how many problems are avoided when this priority is observed? One thing is certain: the likelihood of having disputes and conflicts in your marriage about money and managing material possessions are lessened when the priority plan outlined in the Scriptures is followed step by step.

CHAPTER 2

MONEY AND SPIRITUALITY

In some circles of believers, denying reality about practical material needs seems to be considered a sign of having faith.

The pendulum swings widely to two extremes. First, living as close to the poverty level as possible is seen by some believers as being deeply spiritual. The other side—the one that has risen in popularity with the stardom of prosperity preachers—suggests that the more you have of the world's wealth, the greater the symbol of being blessed by God. Therefore, the higher you climb up the money tree the closer you get to be a spiritual giant.

These extremes deal with the lack of realistic thinking that either poverty or wealth equals spirituality. Yet, according to the Scriptures, both views are foolish.

It is not foolish, however, to consider what the Scriptures say about money, and all other material possessions that represent wealth—with wealth being defined as holding possessions far in excess of what the majority have. In fact, the Lord taught that the measure of one's thinking on material things teaches a great deal about their relationship with Him, and about their eternal destiny.

That does not mean the Lord wants anyone to take the extreme route and turn a deaf ear to hearing about the Christian view of money. Jesus in no way suggested that His followers should ignore material matters. In fact, one of His most interesting statements deals with the subject of facing life on earth from a practical point of view. His teaching actually commended an unbeliever for handling an investment wisely and condemned a believer for being unwise with what he was entrusted.

Managing Material Possessions

This story is told in the parable of the stewards. Two men had assignments to handle possessions for their employers. Jesus carefully noted that the unbeliever did a better job than the believer did. In fact, He made a broad accusation, teaching that overall unbelievers are wiser when handling material matters than believers, known as the children of light.

A practical lesson like this is frequently used to illustrate a spiritual truth in the Scriptures. That does not mean that the original principle should not be practiced, but merely that Christians should be alert to both the practical lesson and the spiritual application. The practical principle should not be neglected in favor of the spiritual lesson any more than the spiritual should be supplanted by the practical. Both have their place in a believer's experience.

When making the spiritual application from Jesus' teaching about the practical wisdom of the unbeliever we learn about faithfully serving the Lord with whatever time, talents, and resources we have. Just as many unjust persons in this world are quite successful in the way they care for earthly concerns, believers ought to be with spiritual matters. And, as the "children of this world" become wise in worldly things, so the "children of light" should seek spiritual wisdom.

However, there is no reason to remove the message of this parable, and the key text cited in particular, from what is really taught. There is no doubt about it. The Lord used this parable of the stewards—one an unbeliever and one a believer—to challenge us about the very practical need to handle money and all other material possessions, wisely.

Regarding the balanced view of money and material things,

the wise man made reasonable and responsible requests of God. Especially important, Solomon asked that he not be left in poverty or riches. Why? Because, if rich he would possibly deny God. And, if he were poor, he feared he would steal and take God's name in vain.

Solomon saw what many believers do not see today—having more than one needs does not draw us closer to God and is not a sign of being blessed. He also understood that there is no special spiritual quality that automatically comes with being poor. Rather, he acknowledged that poverty could press one to the point of acting rashly, even looking at God harshly.

In addition, Solomon recognized that the best thing God could do for anyone would be to let them walk in a path on the course of the balanced Christian life—one where material necessities and spiritual understanding meet and are expressed in the life of a believer who is able to live on earth in ways that honor God.

CHAPTER 3

PRIORITIES FOR CHRISTIANS

Is there a system of priorities for Christians and their money? Is there enough guidance to establish a coherent strategy for our lives? We believe there is, and it can be taught and practiced by any believer who is serious about the truth.

Does God need our money? Does God need anything? If God owns everything, why give?

Since the Scriptures provide sufficient guidance about handling money and other material possessions, what is the first priority? Jesus answered this question centuries ago. He taught that followers of God must put Him first.

What percentage of your income should you set-aside for God first?

We use ten percent in the budgets used in this book. However, how much we present to God creates a more complex decision than merely stating a percentage. For instance, in the Old Testament ten percent was the minimum. In essence, poor or low income Hebrew was to give 10%. Middle class Hebrews gave twenty or thirty percent. The rich gave even more.

Jesus affirmed the tithe in the New Testament. However, Paul later explained that the first coming of Christ and His sacrifice ushered in a new covenant, moving from the demands of the law to the voluntary presentations honored by grace.

Why does God always have to be given the first part? Could it not be just as easily the second tenth? Is it significant that the first tithe was always presented to God?

The issue is not so much which tithe God receives. More important is the matter of priorities.

Giving is part of our relationship with God. That is what He wants. Tithing and giving are part of the ways we honor and worship Him.

How you give when you put God first is a more important issue than how much? . Paul taught that, while not bound by the law, New Testament guidelines for Christian giving teach that it should be:

- Proportionate according to your income
- Consistent, with a regularly scheduled time
- Sacrificial, including giving yourself in service as well as money
- Done cheerfully we are not blessed until we give gladly.

Who Does Not Need To Give?

Unbelievers often charge ministers with just "being after their money." Unfortunately, in some cases, that may be an accurate accusation. What the unbeliever needs to know, however, is that God does not expect them to give to support any form of His work.

According to the New Testament, legitimate ministry deserves support, but the support must be given only by members of the family of God. Early New Testament believers were taught to carefully check out those who claimed to be God's ministers, those who faithfully taught the Word deserved believers' support, and that true believers were to be their only source of support since God did not allow them to take support from unbelievers.

Unbelievers should give to humanitarian causes, and society will honor for that. But they should not be taught or urged to support ministry. When unbelievers are urged to donate to churches and other ministry organizations, their giving will stand in the way of their seeing themselves as sinners who need to be saved. They will argue that their good works should pave the way for them to travel the highway to heaven. But that is not true. Scriptures clearly teach that we are not saved on the basis of our works, but because of the finished work of Christ's sacrifice, burial and resurrection. None are saved by our works — we have nothing to brag about. Salvation is not by our works or righteousness, but because of the mercy and grace of God.

CHAPTER 4

CHRISTIANS AND THEIR MONEY

Money is probably one of the most sensitive subjects that any preacher can discuss. Over the years, when counseling pastors, missionaries, and other spiritual leaders, I've found that most are very hesitant to talk openly about the topic. Too often the issue of compensation creates conflict in pastor/ people relations. Frequently faith missionaries—those who are not related to a denomination and must derive their support directly from individuals and independent churches—fear telling people about their needs. I've known of churches and Christian organizations where God's servants were made to feel guilty for raising questions about what or how they were paid.

Such an attitude is unbiblical; it is one that stands against truth. Paul taught Timothy that "...The labourer is worthy of his reward" (I Tim. 5:18). He was teaching that Christian workers deserve to be appropriately paid. He advanced this argument when defending himself against the unfair accusations of the Corinthians. In I Corinthians 9:7 we read his questions, asked to challenge the Corinthians' charges: "Who goeth a warfare any time at his own charges? Who planted a vineyard, and eateth not of the fruit thereof? Or who feedeth a flock, and eateth not of the milk of the flock?" Paul then drew upon the guidelines for supporting workers that were obvious and had been honored for centuries. He explained that in the Law of Moses it was written: "...Thou shall not muzzle the mouth of the ox that treaded out the corn. Doth God take care for oxen? If we have sown unto you spiritual things, is it a great thing if we shall reap your carnal things?" (I Cor. 9:9, 11).

After identifying his right to be paid, Paul explained that he actually served sacrificially, laying emphasis on the fact that it was a voluntary act (see I Corinthians 9:15-19). He did not teach that anyone else had to make the same decisions regarding service as he did. If they chose to follow Paul's model of sacrifice in ministry, such an act should be voluntary. Therefore, in order for sacrifice to be the quality of sacrifice that honors God, it can only be and must only be voluntary. Forced sacrifice is a demonstration of dishonor—dishonor on the part of those who force others to sacrifice for God's plan. The forced paying of those who serve in spiritual matters may therefore contribute to dishonor among those who are forced to make the sacrifice. Paul set two examples in the open discussion with the Corinthians of his right to receive payment for services. First, he showed all other spiritual leaders that they could and should speak about practical material matters freely. And second, he explained that sacrifice is to be voluntary, not forced.

Another group that finds it difficult to speak openly about money and material matters should be identified. That is the typical married couple. Although disagreement over money is one of the hottest factors that contribute to marital problems among the population in general (and believers are not excepted), facing facts about having money and handling money is still placed on the back burner in most households.

In some circles of believers, denying reality about practical material needs seems to be considered a sign of having faith. Actually, the pendulum swings widely to two extremes. First, living as close to the poverty level as possible is seen by some believers as being deeply spiritual. The other side—the one that has risen in popularity with the stardom of prosperity preachers and their "Ask and you'll receive it" claim—says that the more you have of the world's wealth, the greater the symbol of your being blessed by God and therefore climbing high on the list of spiritual giants. So, the two extremes deal with the unreality of thinking that either poverty or wealth equals spirituality. And, according to the Scriptures, such unreality is actually nonsense and is considered foolish.

It is not foolish, however, to consider what the Scriptures say about money (and all other material possessions that represent wealth)—with wealth being defined as holding possessions far in excess of what the majority have. In fact, the Messiah taught that the measure of one's thinking and emphasis on material things teaches a great deal about their relationship with Him and their eternal destiny. The challenging questions He asked, that are reported in Matthew 16:26, makes this quite clear: "For what is a man profited, if he shall gain the whole world, and lose his own soul? Or what shall a man give in exchange for his soul?" He emphasized His point about prosperity possibly being a stumbling block rather than a stepping stone toward trusting Him with this firm lesson: "Verily I say unto you, that a rich man shall hardly enter into the kingdom of heaven. And again I say unto you. It is easier for a camel to go through the eye of a needle, than for a rich man to enter into the kingdom of God" (Matt. 19:23, 24). And, if we have any question about the meaning of the Messiah's message, it is answered in the disciples' immediate response: "When his disciples heard it, they were exceedingly amazed, saying, who then can be saved?" (Matt. 19:25). There's no doubt about what Jesus was teaching: Riches, wealth, and possessions—or prosperity expressed by any other term—are not likely to encourage or strengthen anyone spiritually. They are more of a hindrance than a help. Jesus said so.

That does not mean that He would have anyone take the extreme route and turn a deaf ear to hearing about the Christian view of money. Jesus in no way suggested that His followers should ignore material matters. In fact, one of the most interesting statements the Messiah ever made deals with the subject of facing life on earth from a practical point of view. In that statement, He actually commended an unbeliever for handling an investment wisely and condemned a believer for being unwise with what was entrusted.

CHAPTER 5

Responsibility for Managing Money

What is the responsibility for managing money?
This story is told in the parable of the stewards,
recorded in Luke, Chapter 16. The key text worthy
of our consideration about how to handle money is Verse 8: "And
the lord commended the unjust steward, because he had done
wisely: for the children of this world are in their generation
wiser than the children of light." Frequently, a practical message
like this is used to illustrate a spiritual truth in the Scriptures.
That does not mean that the original principle should not be
practiced, but merely that Christians should be alert to both
the practical lesson and the spiritual application. The practical
principle should not be neglected in favor of the spiritual lesson
anymore than the spiritual should be supplanted by the practical.
Both should have their place in the believer's experience.

When making the spiritual application from Luke 16:8 we
learn a lesson about faithfully serving the Lord with whatever
time, talent, and resources we have. Just as many unjust persons
in this world are quite successful in the way they care for earthly
concerns, believers ought to be so with spiritual matters. And,
as the "children of this world" become wise in worldly things, so
the "children of light" should seek spiritual wisdom. However,
there is no reason to remove the message of this parable, and
the text cited in particular, from what it is really teaching.
There is no doubt about it, the Messiah used this parable of the
stewards—one an unbeliever and one a believer—to challenge

us about the very practical need to handle money wisely. In fact, not only is the subject of handling money wisely addressed in this parable, we also find the message in many places throughout the Scriptures.

Regarding the balanced view of money or material things, the wise man made this request to God: "Two things have I required of thee; deny me them not before I die: Remove far from me vanity and lies: give me neither poverty nor riches; feed me with food convenient for me: Lest I be full, and deny thee, and say. Who is the LORD? Or lest I be poor, and steal, and take the name of my God in vain" (Prov. 30:7-9). He saw what many believers today do not see—having more than one needs does not draw one closer to God and is not a sign of being blessed. He also understood that there is no special spiritual quality that automatically comes with being poor. In fact, he acknowledged that poverty could press one to the point of acting rashly, even of looking at God harshly. Rather, the wise man recognized that the best thing God could do for anyone would be to let him walk in a path on the course of the balanced Christian life—one where material necessities and spiritual understanding meet and are expressed in the life of the believer who is able to live on earth in ways that honor God.

How to Become Wealthy

Before we dig too deeply into the Word, let me give you one simple lesson for becoming wealthy. It has nothing to do with magical formulas. It has nothing to do with get-rich-quick schemes. And, it is equally applicable for a born-again believer, for the most blatant unbelievers, or for anyone in between. It will work satisfactorily for anyone.

But before I give this sure-fire, wealth-building factor, I must tell you that it is very simple. In fact, it is so simple that you may wonder why I'm telling you. It is surely something that you have thought about once or twice. It's got to be something that you already know. Just the same, I promised to mention it—so I will.

Here is the guaranteed principle for creating wealth. There are three parts to the plan, and each must be rigidly observed. First, you must spend less than you earn. Second, you must start saving early. Third, you must save regularly. Anyone who sets this principle in motion—assuming that instead of putting your savings under the mattress you invest them in some financial programs that produce earnings—will, in time, create wealth.

Now, do not think for one minute that I'm being unfaithful to what the Bible teaches about what to do with your money. According to some "prosperity" preachers who twist truth and teach mystical plans for getting everything you want by just claiming it, the practical teaching that I offer—though it is biblical truth—may seem unspiritual, unscriptural and very dull. My disagreement with most of them has nothing to do with thoughts that God cannot do anything that He chooses to do, including providing material things such as better jobs and more money. My disagreement is that they fail to acknowledge one basic fact. The truth is this: No one has ever created wealth without learning how to handle money wisely, nor without applying what they have learned.

If you will seriously consider what the Word of God really says, you will see that the formula I have supplied is firmly founded on scriptural teaching. In the Proverbs we have instructions about the wisdom of preparing for the future. The illustration is drawn from—of all creatures—ants! We would normally just consider them annoying, but God says that they have wisdom that believers could well discover. "Go to the ant, consider her ways, and be wise: Which having no guide, overseer, or ruler, provides her meat in the summer, and gathers her food in the harvest" (Proverbs. 6:6-8). It is easy to see that the spiritual application teaches about preparing for eternity, but the practical interpretation is clearly a message about wisely handling material things today in anticipation of the needs of tomorrow.

So the twofold lesson from the ants teaches about planning for tomorrow. It presents a spiritual message and clearly presents practical truth about financial planning. Let me re-emphasize, then, in no uncertain terms: The way to have more tomorrow than you have today is to spend less today than you earn. Then you must set aside the difference between what you earn and what you spend in savings. Besides that, you must invest in something that gives your savings earning power so that what you save will increase.

Remember, the unjust steward of Jesus' parable was commended because he handled the investment that was entrusted to him wisely. So one of the first lessons that believers must pay attention to regarding handling money is the one that teaches us to handle it wisely. Do you know how to handle money wisely? And, if you know how, do you practice what you know? In Romans 12:11 Paul taught this: Be "Not slothful in business'," And the wise man who wrote the practical lessons found in the Book of Proverbs said: "The hand of the diligent shall bear rule: but the slothful shall be under tribute" (Prov. 12:24). It is evident, when we study the Scriptures seriously, that paying proper attention to material matters is neither unscriptural nor unspiritual. The truth is, more believers need to order their lives and observe the biblically-sanctioned balance between thoughtful handling of material matters and maintaining careful concern for their spiritual well-being.

Chapter 6

A Biblical View of Prosperity

Much has been taught in recent years by some ministers about believers enjoying prosperity. They have supported their teachings with proof-texts that at first reading may seem to say that God wants everyone to be wealthy. If you listen to the modern ministers who talk as though they are dedicated to every believer having lots of money—especially themselves—some may sound like they have a better plan than what the Bible really teaches. Unfortunately, the undiscerning is readily taken in by the prosperity preacher's private interpretation of a Bible verse or two.

Some preachers even seem to say that believers who are not well-to-do, or at least aren't headed in that direction, must lack faith. The idea is that not having plenty in your pocketbook is a pretty good sign that you're probably guilty of sin.

Well, that sounds pretty scary; and since almost everyone I know would like to have more, and since no one is perfect, the shoe of that message fits the foot of every believer I know. Do you see the easy and twisted message that prosperity preachers have to preach? How much is enough? When do we not want more than we have? Is the old nature ever satisfied to the fullest? When you come up with sensible answers to questions like these, you see why the minister who preaches that you ought to have more money always finds a mind that matches that message.

And if you ever meet the person who could not find some

sin that might be clogging up the channel of blessing to keep him from being as prosperous as he wants to be, then you'll either be dreaming or already in Heaven walking on street of gold. You see, the fact is, no one is perfect while on earth-no one is sinless. Therefore, if a particular sin is what keep your pockets from bulging with bounty from somewhere, then you'd never have a chance to enjoy material blessings and you'd never meet anyone who ever had more than anyone else—at least not enough for anybody to notice.

There may really be an element of greed and hasty gain in the typical message about material prosperity. How sad it is that Christians would be caught in that trap! In Proverb; 28:20 we are told this: "A faithful man shall abound with blessings: but he that makes haste to be rich shall not be innocent" (the marginal rendering for "innocent" reads "or unpunished"). Proverbs 21:5 teaches that "The thoughts of the diligent tend only to plenteousness; but of every one that is hasty only to want" And in Chapter 20, Verse 21 of the same book that is filled with such practical instructions, we are taught: "An inheritance may be gotten hastily at the beginning; but the end thereof shall not be blessed" Finally, the same word that describes the true story of many is told: "He that it greedy of gain troubles his own house;..." (Prov. 15:27) So, while prosperity preaching rings well in the ears of those who rush for earthly riches (even doing so under a religious banner), the truth is that the unadulterated, though less-exciting and less-glittering, message from God's Word is that such material gain may really equal spiritual loss.

Count Your Blessings That Count

Twentieth-century believers don't really know how to measure God's blessings very well. In fact, most don't even know how to determine what are and what are not God's blessings. You see, we all have the tendency to decide that only the things that make us feel good, look better, or material things that add up to "more" are in the category of blessings. But God figures differently. And those who know Him well come to appreciate in time that even some things that aren't usually counted as blessings really are. For instance, Paul told the believers in Philippi: "...unto you it is given in the behalf of Christ, not only to believe on him, but also to suffer for his sake" (Phil. 1:29). And the Holy Spirit reports through Dr. Luke that the Apostles, after being put in jail, beaten, and commanded not to speak the name of Jesus, rejoiced "...that they were counted worthy to suffer shame for his name" (Acts 5:41; see Verses 17-42).

I've never heard anybody do much preaching and teaching about the blessings of being imprisoned or beaten. But then, I've not heard via the media or met anyone personally who would be of the early New Testament Christian variety either. The point is this: Few modern believers have the spiritual discernment to recognize some blessings. Believers who are caught up in the prosperity craze may consider things like money, stocks and bonds, big houses and cars blessings when, in fact, they may be a snare! When Paul warned Timothy about one of the devil's snares, he made this clear: "But they that will be rich fall into temptation and a snare, and into many foolish and hurtful lusts, which drown men in destruction and perdition. But thou, o man of God, flee these things; and follow after righteousness, godliness, faith, love, patience, meekness...godliness with contentment is great gain. For we brought nothing into this world, and it is certain we can carry nothing out. And having food and raiment let us be therewith content" (I Tim. 6:9, 11, 6-8). The things that eyes which are blind to spiritual truth, see as blessings may well be the great barriers to true dedication. Be careful!

Chapter 7

Budgeting: More Spiritual Than Many Think

Now, let us move into an area that is extremely practical. It is somewhat personal, and more than that, it could be downright touchy. But, I want this study to be helpful. And it will not be if I approach the subject of material things, of money, and spiritualize everything. In order to be practical about this important theme, I must raise some questions. For instance, do you have a budget? One of the most helpful tools that any household can have is a budget. It should not be a set of rules that bind, but a good guide to help you through the maze of monetary matters. Everyone should have some sort of budget. If you don't have a budget, you are not likely to know where your money needs to go; and without a budget, when the money is gone, you probably won't know too well where it went! Having a budget is one of the basic ways for handling money wisely; it is a sign that you want to be a good steward.

Someone has said: "If your outgo is greater than your income, your upkeep is in for a downfall." How true. And many dedicated believers know this. A good budget will let you know about your outgo and your income; it will advise you about the cost of your upkeep and be a guide to prevent you from experiencing a downfall.

One biblical instruction about the value of budgeting is found in another one of Jesus' messages where He drew from a practical case dealing with material things to illustrate a spiritual truth. In Luke 14:28-30 we read this: "For which of you, intending to build a tower, sitteth not down first, and counteth the cost, whether he has sufficient to finish it? Lest haply, after he hath laid the foundation, and is not able to finish it, all that behold it begin to mock him, Saying, This man began to build, and was not able to finish"

We need not wonder about the rich spiritual lesson the Messiah wanted to impress upon the minds of His hearers with this message. That is explained in Verse 33: "So likewise, whosoever he is of you that forsake not all that he hath, he cannot be my disciple" (Luke 14:33). When the Messiah talked about a tower builder who didn't make sufficient plans regarding the cost of his project—who didn't create a budget—His primary message was an emphasis upon the cost of discipleship. It costs believers nothing to be saved—that cost Christ His life—but it does cost us something to be disciples, to be real Christians.

However, as already noted, when a spiritual truth is illustrated by using a practical message that does not change the practical side of the story at all. In fact, it strengthens the role of the practical, for if the practical teaching was not solid it could not be well used to convey a strong spiritual lesson. So, although from the spiritual teaching we understand that the Messiah's primary point in this story was to stress the cost of discipleship, He based the whole message on the fact that wise people don't jump into projects without seriously considering the cost. And He made the point well that the person who plans to finish what he started, from a material and practical point of view, will lay plans, make prudent projections, and will establish a budget that explains where he is financially, and suggests where he can or cannot go in the future. A budget is one of the best guides anyone can have for walking in a right practical direction. Still, many Christians do not have a budget, and some do not know how to create one. Therefore, here is a sample that may be helpful.

Monthly Budget Example for Christians

INCOME:

Head of Household	$	_____
Spouse (If Applicable)	+	_____
Interest Income	+	_____
Other Income (Rental, Business, etc.)	+	_____
TOTAL GROSS INCOME	$	_____

EXPENSES:

House Payments (Mortgage/Rent)	$	_____
Property Taxes (If Not Included in Pymt.)	+	_____
Home Insurance (If Not Included in Pymt.)	+	_____
Home Maintenance (Repairs)	+	_____
Car Loan(s)	+	_____
Utilities	+	_____
Auto Insurance	+	_____
Health Insurance (If Applicable)	+	_____
Life Insurance (If Applicable)	+	_____
Other Installment Loans (Boat, R.V.)	+	_____
Charge Card Payments	+	_____
Auto Operating Costs (Gas, Oil, Tune-ups)	+	_____
Food	+	_____
Meals Away from Home	+	_____
Family Expenses (Medical, Dental)	+	_____
Clothing	+	_____
Entertainment	+	_____
Miscellaneous (Gifts, Newspaper, Cable TV)	+	_____
Contributions to Ministries	+	_____
Contributions to Charities	+	_____
TOTAL EXPENSES	$	_____

SAVINGS:

IRA (Husband)	$	_____

IRA (Wife)   + _____
Pension Contribution   + _____
Savings Account Deposit   + _____
Emergency Fund Deposit   + _____
Education Fund Deposit (If Applicable)   + _____
TOTAL SAVINGS CONTRIBUTION $ _____
Total Net Income: $ _____
Total Expenses: - _____
Total Savings Contribution: - _____
TOTAL SURPLUS OR (DEFICIT) $ _____

More Month than Money

If your budget shows a monthly surplus, you are being a good steward of your income. If you regularly show a deficit, you are in financial trouble and must make some adjustments. That means that you will have to give up some things. You should carefully consider how to reduce some of your expenses. People often overlook some of the easiest ways to lower expenses. For instance, reevaluate your insurance programs, especially on insurances for automobile and property. This requires shopping around, and that takes time and energy. But the ultimate outcome may show a sizeable savings and help lift some of the financial burden. You may be over insured. Why pay for insurance that you do not need?

Questions about Auto Insurance

1. Are you the only driver of the insured car?
2. Have you had any accidents in the past three years?
3. If "Yes," were you at fault?
4. Have you ever been at fault in an accident?
5. Is your car fully paid for?
6. If you answered "Yes" to 1 & 5, "No" to 2, 3 & 4, do you really need to pay for comprehensive and collision coverage?
7. Would liability and uninsured motorist coverage satisfy your auto insurance needs?

If you answered "Yes" to 1, 5 & 7, "No" to 2, 3, 4 & 6, the sooner you change your auto insurance the more money you will save. If you answered "Yes" to 1 & 5, "No" to 2, 3 & 4, but are uncertain about your answers for 6 & 7, you should discuss your auto insurance needs with a financial consultant and then your auto insurance agent.

Questions about Life Insurance

1. Do you pay premiums on a whole life insurance policy?

2. Are you using insurance as a savings instrument?

3. Are you a parent with dependents at home?

4. Are you a parent with grown children?

5. Do you own the house where you live?

6. Is your home fully paid for?

7. Does anyone need a sizeable inheritance from you to sustain him/her?

8. Do you have any large outstanding debts that need to be protected by insurance?

If you answered "Yes" to 1, 2, 3, 5, 7 & 8, you need insurance but you may want to get an insurance checkup. The same coverage could probably be purchased for much less by purchasing the kind of insurance that best serves its primary purpose, that of providing death benefits to beneficiaries, not as a savings account.

If you answered "Yes" to 6, "Yes" or "No" to 4, you may be wise to discuss your actual insurance needs with a financial consultant and/or your insurance agent. Unless you intend to leave large amounts of money to adult children, there is little reason to pay insurance premiums on policies payable to them. Depending on circumstances and desires, in later years burial insurance may be the only type actually needed.

Another simple but important way to adjust your budget is to make sure that you do not yield to impulse spending. Paul taught the Thessalonians to "Pray without ceasing" (I Thessalonians. 5:17). Some think that means to be praying all the time, or at least to be in what they call an "attitude of prayer" all the time. Frankly, referring to the "attitude of prayer" makes praying something that is done only when you feel a certain way, or look a particular way, or perhaps both. Granted, there are times when a believer will "feel" more like praying than at others. However, that does not mean that no prayer should be offered if and when you don't have that certain "feeling." And I do not believe that is what Paul taught anyway. His message spoke to the fact that believers should not enter into an activity or thought that could not be comfortably accompanied by prayer. Believers who took time to pray about what otherwise would be a purchase by impulse would save a lot of money. They would also find that they would not make purchases for a lot of things that they do not need. The idea of praying about every purchase moves a step forward toward another helpful guard against unwise spending, against impulse buying.

Establish the rule of waiting before buying—a few minutes, a few hours, or a few days. You will purchase less and therefore spend less. But you will also have more—more peace of mind, more money in hand, more satisfaction experienced by people who handle money wisely.

People who are away from home at mealtime—many of us are away from the house at lunchtime—can save money by carrying a bag lunch. That may be an uneasy adjustment to make, but "brown bagging it" will save a bundle. And when there are deficits—when the outgo is greater than the income—adjusting one's eating habits can help lift the burden that monthly financial deficit brings.

Change Your Credit

One of the most obvious ways to reduce expenses is by regulating credit purchases. People who live by credit cards constantly court financial trouble. You can cut your problem spending radically by throwing away the credit cards, leaving them in a place where it is difficult to get to them, or by simply exercising the discipline that dictates that only emergency purchases will be made by credit card. I am sorry that some radio and TV preachers urge people to use their charge cards to make contributions to their ministries; that are not in the best interest of the credit card holder. In fact, the high interest rates charged for cash advances on credit cards makes credit card contributions more of a burden for the giver than a blessing.

The Bible has much to say against making purchases on credit. In Proverbs 22:26 we read this warning: "Be not thou one of them that strike hands, or of them that are sureties for debts" Paul taught the same message in the New Testament:

Is debt evil? No. Is debt a sin? No. Is debt used appropriately? No. If debt were utilized appropriately, there would be almost no bankruptcies, repossessions, foreclosures and marital problems related to finances. Some people just can't resist creating debt. It seems as though they become addicted to borrowing, especially by using credit cards. People who have to purchase on credit what should be paid for by cash are in deep trouble. Credit card spending or creating credit by making a contribution is not the sign of a wise steward.

Chapter 8

When You Need Help

People who do well in life are accustomed to seeking advice from others. We all know individuals who won't seek or take advice—you can't tell them anything because they think they know everything. But, according to the Bible, such people are very foolish. In Proverbs 12:15 we are told that "The way of a fool is right in his own eyes: but he that hearkened unto counsel is wise." So those who truly succeed in life are smart enough to accept that they do not know everything; their intelligence alerts them to the need for help from others who are especially informed on specific issues, including financial matters. The Bible teaches that those who do not seek counsel fall; Scriptures make it clear that "Without counsel purposes are disappointed: but in the multitude of counselors there is safety" (see Proverbs 11:14; 15:22).

It is certainly right to seek counsel when (1) you do not know what you should know about financial matters; (2) you cannot create a budget; or (3) you cannot control your spending. According to Proverbs 1:5, "A wise man will hear, and will increase learning; and a man of understanding shall attain unto wise counsels." Receiving solid advice may help the person who is struggling with financial problems discover ways of correcting his/her situation. Of course, for anyone who is not accustomed to dealing with others in the area of financial concerns, there is the question of finding someone who is qualified to help.

Bad Counsel

In any field where counseling is offered there are people who will provide bad advice, just as there are those who render valuable consultation services. Identifying them is the costly concern. Interestingly, the Word of God supplies some general guidelines to follow for finding qualified counselors, no matter what their area. In the case of professions in the field of finance you may encounter people who are accountants, various types of bank officers, financial planners and others who may provide advice for a fee. Although you may think so, the fee is not the most important factor to consider; the quality of advice is more important.

One of the first guidelines to follow when you need counsel is presented in the Old Testament Book of I Kings, Chapter 12. Israel's King Rehoboam was pressed by the people of the kingdom to tell them how he was going to treat them. "Thy father made our yoke grievous:" they told him, "now therefore make thou the grievous service of thy father, and his heavy yoke which he put upon us, lighter, and we will serve thee" (I Kings 12:4). Before answering them the King wanted some time to think. He told the people that he would give them an answer within three days (see I Kings 12:5). During that time he "...consulted with the old men that stood before Solomon his father...and said, how do ye advise that I may answer this people? And they spoke unto him, saying, If thou wilt be a servant unto this people this day, and wilt serve them, and answer them, and speak good words to them, then they will be thy servants for ever" (I Kings 12:6, 7).

The proud new and young rebellious King didn't like that advice. "But he forsook the counsel of the old men,...and consulted with the young men that were grown up with him,... And [they]...spoke unto him, saying, Thus shall thou speak unto this people...My little finger shall be thicker than my father's loins. And now whereas my father did lade you with a heavy yoke, I will add to your yoke: my father hath chastised you with whips, but I will chastise you with scorpions" (I Kings 12:8, 10, and 11). The result of King Rehoboam's rejecting the counsel of the old men and responding to the advice from those who were his own age, the young men, was that the kingdom was divided. Bad counsel is always costly and, as in the case with King Rehoboam, bad counsel is likely to be the message that we want to hear, not what we need to hear. It is the most expensive advice one can receive.

How to Find a Good Consultant

The principle that clearly stands out is that when you want good advice, seek it from someone with experience. This is basic in the search for a helpful consultant on any matter, but especially in the area of handling your money.

Another issue is the self-interest of the person sought to be your financial counselor. If the person who advises you about how to handle your money has something personal to gain from what he or she tells you—other than the gain of reasonable compensation paid for consulting service—you need to be alert and weigh his or her words carefully. It is not unreasonable to pay a professional consultant for advice about money matters, but advisors with financial products to sell may be swayed to think more of what is good for them than for you. What they offer may be good, but if the benefit tilts in the direction of the one who makes the offer, it may not be in your best interest.

King Rehoboam received both good and bad counsel. The good counsel came from the old men who had the best interest of the people at heart. They had the experience of working with the people for many years and saw the burdens they bore that were placed on them by Rehoboam's father. It was obviously not in the self-interest of the older and experienced men to give the young King advice that he didn't want to hear. In contrast, the young men had little, if any experience, but a great deal of self-interest for the recommendations that they made. When these two factors are prominent—lack of experience and self-interest, those who seek counsel should listen to their advisors and weigh their words with caution.

What Do Those Letters Mean?

One appropriate way to evaluate a counselor in any field is to check out their credentials. This is a practice that most people do not follow, although it is one that was observed again and again in biblical times. For instance, when Nehemiah responded to God's call to leave his post as the King's cupbearer and return to lead in rebuilding the walls of Jerusalem, he made this request: "...If it please the king, let letters be given me to the governors beyond the river, that they may convey me over till I come into Judah; And a letter unto Asaph the keeper of the king's forest, that he may give me timber to make beams for the gates of the palace..." (Neh. 2:7, 8). In other words, Nehemiah wanted his King to issue information that documented his credentials that authenticated his right to do what he did.

Letters of approval, letters that spoke to his "credentialing" or right to act were also part of the plan for New Testament churches during the days of the Apostle Paul. Regarding faithful people who would carry the offering gathered from churches to help the suffering saints in Jerusalem, Paul taught this practice to the Corinthians: "Upon the first day of the week let every one of you lay by him in store, as God hath prospered him, that there be no gatherings when I come. And when I come, whomsoever ye shall approve by your letters, them will I send to bring your liberality unto Jerusalem" (I Cor. 16:2, 3). Asking information about the credentials of someone you do not know was an accepted and probably expected practice in both Old Testament and New Testament times (see Nehemiah 6:17, 19; Acts 9:2; 22:5). It is a practice that is highly recommended today when you seek someone for counsel. When dealing with financial consultants, knowing about credentials may give information about the type and quality of advice you will receive.

Credentials merely suggest that someone has studied and therefore should be better informed than others in a given area. Today, there are several credentials that may identify someone who has seriously studied in areas that would enable him or her to offer financial advice. These include a college degree or degrees, such as a B.S., an M.B.A. (representing a higher degree of study), and a Ph.D. (the highest degree that is awarded in any academic field of study)—from a program in business studies. (Majors could include accounting, finance, economics, or business administration.)

Also, there are professional designations that say that the person holding them has engaged in specific areas of study offered by a recognized agency serving the field of business of the special disciplines of accounting, insurance, finance, economics, or even direct studies in financial planning (C.EA. = Certified Public Accountant; C.F.R = Certified Financial Planner; Ch.EC. = Chartered Financial Consultant). These credentials are not awarded just because somebody joins a professional organization! They are granted to the individuals holding them after being tested, either by a state agency or by an institution that offers coursework in specific studies. Passing the appropriate tests demonstrates being knowledgeable in the areas of expertise that the credentials address.

Valid credentials held by professionals today serve a purpose similar to the letters of recommendation and approval for people in biblical times. People who want good financial advice will check credentials and find a consultant who can put into words of advice what years of study and experience have taught.

The Ultimate Counsel

Now, there is one source for counsel that we must not forsake—a source that certainly should not be supplanted by any other. Rather, we should evaluate all other counsel about matters in life, including financial matters, with the Word from God as revealed in the Scriptures. Although the Bible is the primary source from which we are given this counsel, it is expressed to us in diverse ways, such as through understanding given to us by the Holy Spirit (see I Corinthians 2:9-14; Ephesians 4:18-32; I John 2:27), through other believers (see Ephesians 4:11, 12; Hebrews 3:13), and through experience (see I Corinthians 16:9; II Corinthians 2:12; Colossians 4:3; Revelation 3:8). For believers, valid and valued counsel will be weighed by the teachings of God's Word.

Failure to listen to God was a frequent fault of God's Chosen People. The Psalmist reported His complaint against them: "But my people would not hearken to my voice; and Israel would none of me. So I gave them up unto their own hearts' lust: and they walked in their own counsels. Oh that my people had hearkened unto me, and Israel had walked in my ways!" (Psalm 81:11-13). They missed being blessed, both materially and spiritually, because they turned a deaf ear to God's counsel and walked in their own.

Believers need to remember the words of the wise man who said, "Trust in the LORD with all thine heart; and lean not unto thine own understanding. In all thy ways acknowledge him, and he shall direct thy paths" (Prov. 3:5, 6).

When Christians think about money, whether about the money we have or about the money we need, God is also interested. In what we call "The Lord's Prayer," the Messiah taught that God has thought and done something about our material needs even before we knew we had them, and before we asked Him about them (see Matthew 6:8). While we tend to think in terms of His concern for our spiritual welfare, the Bible teaches that He cares about our practical needs too. His Word is a lamp and a light along every path of life, including the one marked by financial decisions (see Psalm 119:105; Philippians 4:6, 7, 19).

Some people make the mistake of claiming that "money is the root of all evil." Paul taught that "...the love of money is the root of all evil:..." (I Tim. 6:10). Note: he said, "The love of money," not "the money." How Christians handle money provides good evidence of how and what they think about money.

Without doubt, the message Christians should ponder when thinking about money is the one Jesus taught: "But seek ye first the kingdom of God and his righteousness; and all these things shall be added unto you" (Matt. 6:33).

CHAPTER 9

Christian Financial Decision Making: Debunking the Myths

If there are over 2,000 verses on money, what subject does the Bible have more to say on? If there are any material resources under your control over influence, what do you do with them? Will you answer to God for the way you managed your financial resources?

The First Part Goes To God

Why? Does God need our money? What are the first fruits? How much are you required to give? To whom? In what way? When? In what spirit, does God want giving? What are some foundations verses requiring a tithe?

Old Testament Tithing.

Genesis 14:18-21 Abraham tithed worship, Melchizedek.
Deuteronomy 14:23 Tithe of corn. wine. oil. first animals.
2 Samuel 24:24 Shall I offer that which costs me nothing.
Isaiah 40:8 Things cannot change the Word of God.
Psalm 16:7-8 Word cannot be shaken
Psalm 62 God is my priority
Proverbs 1:7 Fear of Lord beginning knowledge.
Proverbs 3:9 Honor the Lord with your substance.
Proverbs 3:10 So shall your barns be filled plenty.

Haggai 2:8 All wealth belongs to God.

Malachi 3:8-11 God will open the windows of Heaven.

Old Testament Time Period Reported in New Testament:

Matthew 20:35 Heaven and earth will pass away.

Matthew 21:12 Jesus overthrew moneychangers.

Matthew 23:23 Pharisees paid tithes.

Matthew 24:45-46 Blessed is servant, Lord finds faithful.

Matthew 25:33-40 Hungry and you fed me.

Mark 10:29 Receive hundred fold.

Mark 12:42-44 Motive in giving.

Luke 6:38 Give and it shall be given you.

Luke 12:16 Abundant life.

Luke 21:1-4 Widow's mite.

John 14:6 I am the way, the truth, and the life.

New Testament Giving.

James 2:15-16 If brother be destitute of daily food.

1 John 3:17-18 Who so has world's goods, sees brother.

2 Corinthians 8:7-9 Abundant life.

Hebrews 13:16 To communicate, forget not, God pleased.

John 3:18-19 Light comes into the world, condemned.

Romans 11:3 Or who has first given to him.

Hebrews 7:1-10 Melchizedek blessed Abraham.

Hebrews 12:27 Cannot be shaken.

Romans 8 Nothing can separate us from the love.

2 Corinthians 8:14 Equality in giving and sharing.

1 Corinthians 9:9 Not muzzle the ox with the corn.

3 John 5-6 Charity before the church.

1 Corinthians 9:14 Preachers should get paid.

Giving to the poor.

Do the poor qualify for these gifts?

Proverbs 3:27 Withhold not good when it is in your power.

Proverbs 11:24 There is that scatters, yet increases.

Proverbs 11:25 Liberal soul shall be made fat.

Proverbs 21:26 He covets greedily, but righteous gives.

Deuteronomy 15:11 Open hand wide poor and needy.

Matthew 25:45 Did to least of them.

Luke 3:11 Two coats, give one. Meat same.

Proverbs 21:20 Treasure dwelling wise, foolish spends.

1 Corinthians 13:13 Faith, hope, charity.

Romans 15:26 Contribution to the poor saints.

Luke 12:33 Sell all have, give alms to kingdom.

Proverbs 25:21 If your enemy be hungry, give bread.

Proverbs 28:27 He that gives to the poor shall not lack.

Matthew 25:36 Naked and clothed me, Hungry and.

Matthew 5:42 Give to him that asks of you.

Matthew 10:42 Cup of cold water to little ones.

CHAPTER 10

HOW TO GIVE

Is it materialistic to discuss money in church? The answer is yes, an emphatic yes. Any subject discussed in the Word of God must surely be discussed in His church. How many occasions does the Bible address financial issues? Some have suggested that over 2,000 references exist. What subject does the Bible have more to say on? There are certainly fewer verses on Sin, Heaven and many so called spiritual topics combined. Regarding material resources under your control or influence, what does God want you to do with them? Does God have a plan for you and your resources? Will you answer to God for the way you managed your financial resources? If we are accountable for various decisions and actions, we must surely be accountable in the subject area representing the greatest number of decisions and actions.

Is there a system of priorities for a Christian? Is there enough guidance to establish a coherent strategy for our lives? We think there is, and feel we can lay it out for any believer truly seeking the truth. If there is sufficient guidance, what is the first priority? And, is there a verse suggesting so? Seek you first the kingdom of God and His righteousness, and all these things shall be added unto you. Matthew 6:25-40. What percentage? In the budgets in this book, 10 percent is used. However, it is a far more complex decision than merely stating a percentage.

In the Old Testament, 10% was the minimum. In essence, poor or low income Hebrews were to give 10%. Middle class

Hebrews gave 20 or 30%, and the rich gave even a higher percentage. In the New Testament, Jesus reaffirmed the tithe. However, Paul explained later that we are under grace and not under the law. More on that later, but back to the tithe itself.

Why does it always have to be the first part? Could it not be just as easily the second tenth? Is it significant that it is always the first tenth? It appears to be more a matter of one's priorities. And why the tithe anyway? Does God need our money? Haggai 2:8. The silver is mine and the gold is mine, says the Lord of Hosts. Does God need anything? Does God want anything? If God owns all the wealth of the believers and all the wealth of the unbelievers, why give? Because the giver is the one blessed. Why give of ourselves? Because we are blessed. Our attitude? Our attitude begins to change for the better. God wants a relationship with us. God wants to bless us with happiness. That is why giving and tithing must be part of our worship of Him.

Mark 7:6. He answered and said unto them. Well has Isaiah prophesied of you hypocrites; as it is written the people honor me with their lips, but their heart is far from me. Tithing is nothing to brag about. Tithing does not make one spiritual. No more than church attendance or fidelity to one's spouse. It is one of many aspects of the Christian life.

Mark 4:19. And what of the well known parable of sowing seed with different results (responses)? This passage relates to our response to the Word of God. This author fails to see that there is any financial principle to be drawn. Yet, it tends to be included in some sermons on tithing.

Mark 10:23. It is easier for a rich man to enter the eye of a needle, than to enter the kingdom of Heaven. With riches alone, no man can enter Heaven, but with Christ all things are possible. We want to believe that professional sports athletes, movie stars, politicians and other famous people are saved. Why? Jesus said very few rich people are going to Heaven. And, what are the first fruits? Our Lord is saying there are some aspects of life which are more important than money.

Putting God first. How much are you required to give?

Are we under grace. If so, how can a percentage be stated

accurately for all believers? To whom do we give? Only to certain individuals and groups. It seems that the Lord would be able to remember who he wanted to list. If the group or individual is not in the New Testament lists, how can we in good conscience, give them anything? For example, the United Way is not one of the designated groups.

Yet, believers across this nation give to these groups. I hope they do not count those donations as part of their tithe!

In what way do we contribute? As a part of our worship. This eliminates-almost all giving to ministries we are not directly connected to. If I give to a group in another state, I must have a strong and direct relationship with that group, either through a personal history or diligent prayer. To give to some disconnected organization however spiritual they may seem, simply has no Biblical basis. When do we give? When we worship. There was never any New Testament giving apart from worship.

In what spirit, does God want giving? Cheerfully. Many give from fear or pride or obligation. Jesus said these religious people have their reward. In other words, there is no spiritual blessing if money is given without a cheerful attitude and a contrite and worshipful heart.

What are some foundation verses requiring a tithe? What was the first quotation in the Old Testament on Tithing? Genesis 4:3 and in the process of time Sabbath day Cain brought of the fruit of the ground an offering unto the Lord. worship Hebrews 11:4 by faith, Abel offered unto God a more excellent sacrifice than Cain by which he obtained witness that he was righteous God testifying of his gifts and by it being dead yet speaks. Here is a tithe before the Mosaic law.

Genesis 14:18-21 Cain knew what God expected. How did he know? Did Adam and Eve know? Of course, we have the advantage of the Bible.

And Melchizedek king of Salem brought forth bread and wine and he was the priest of the most high god and he blessed him and said blessed be Abraham of the most high god possessor of heaven and earth and blessed be the most high god which has delivered your enemies in to your hand and he gave him tithes of all communion he had and the king of Sodom said unto Abraham give the persons and take the goods to yourself cultural but not scriptural. Twice in Scripture, we are instructed not to tithe from something that came to us freely. Gambling, lottery, and Bingo winnings, represent types of income, where there could be no spiritual blessing from tithing.

What does Deuteronomy 12:6 say about: Burnt offerings? (Anything in return?) There would be nothing left of value to salvage. Sacrifices? (Praise?) There are many sacrifices and they do not always involve money. Tithes? (No control?) When you give to the church, you have no more control over the money. Heave offerings? There are times when others should be involved in the praise of God at the time of your giving. Vows? (Commitments?) We are warned never to vow without a serious appraisal of the obligation. Jesus said count the cost. Freewill offerings? First fruits?

Deuteronomy 15:11. You shall open your hand wide to your brother, to your poor, to your needy, in your hand. Is tithing more than money? Deuteronomy 14:23 How much sharing do we see today? Who really cares about the poor? God does. God cares more than we do. And much of what is done for the poor comes as a result of individuals and groups who may have been led by what God thinks we should be doing for the poor.

What do these symbols represent? Corn? Word of God. Wine? Spiritual power. What is the significance of the word first? In verse 28, did they pay three tithes or 30%?

What gifts to the Lord constitute a tithe? 2 Samuel 24:24 In the story of Araunah, and his offer of a gift to David. David said shall I give that which cost nothing?

Some have recommended to parents, that they not give money to their children to tithe. This undermines what we should be teaching children about tithing. It must be sacrificial or it cannot be part of worship. Far better to involve them by letting them place your envelope in the offering plate or basket. This way they know it cost something. This way they know it is not a game to trick God, but rather an expression of service and worship. Yes, Job made sacrifices for his adult children, but in the context of asking forgiveness for their sins. However, I think if the parent explains giving to a child, the child will learn to understand the parent.

What did the Lord promise the Jewish people concerning tithing and their material prosperity?

Proverbs 3:9-10. Honor the lord with your substance and with the first fruits of all your increase so shall your barns be filled with plenty and your presses shall burst out with new wine. If it disappoints you to know that you will not be wealthy if you come to Christ. Oh, one tenth of one percent of Christians will be very rich. However, your statistical odds of being rich are better if you are not saved. The Devil is the prince of this world. If money is all that is needed to keep you from Heaven, Satan will arrange it for you.

Proverbs 3:27. Withhold not good from them to whom it is due, when it is in the power of your hand to do it. How well do you tip waiters, waitresses, taxi drivers, and bellhops and valets? If you are not among the best tippers, please do not pray in their restaurant or witness or display a Christian bumper sticker. Every time you cheat a poor unbeliever out of their rightful reward, you displease God and cause harm to our efforts to teach the World about Christ. If your church group eats in a restaurant, do not tell them who you are with, unless you are prepared to tip well. And many churches have deacons, and elders who have. prospered by cheating the less fortunate. Their tithes and offerings cannot compensate for how they obtained their money. For example, most people were deceived into purchasing whole life or universal life insurance. Some Christian may have sold it to them. Even if a Christian lies and deceives the Bible condemns their tithes and offerings. Jesus criticized the Jewish religious leaders for abusing the poor. Is it the American way? Yes, but it is not the Christian way. Can one be wealthy in an honorable way? Yes, it can be done, if God wants you to be in that small group of rich people.

Proverbs 11:24-26. There is that scatters, and yet increases, and there is that withholds more than is meet but it tends to poverty. The liberal soul shall be made fat and he that waters shall be watered also himself, he that withholds corn, the people shall curse him: but blessing shall be upon the head of him that sells it. There is a general principle in scripture that you are rewarded algebraically and exponentially for what you give. The rewards are generally material in nature in the New Testament and generally spiritually in nature in the Old Testament. Joseph, Nabal, David and Abigail are some characters who come to mind regarding corn. Corn is also the Word of God, in some segments of Scripture.

Malachi 3:8-11 What is stored in Heaven which can be poured out on earth? Could it be fruits of the spirit? Does God store dollar bills in Heaven? Why would He? If God has no money in Heaven, what blessings is he pouring out? What earthly treasure would God store in Heaven? It is ridiculous to think that God is a slot machine. If I give him $100, he will pay me back $1,000. If that were true, the Church would be the largest investment brokerage in the history of mankind!

In terms of material blessings to the Hebrews, is there a verse in the Gospels that makes the same promise to the church? No. Is there a verse in the New Testament that makes the same promise to the church? No. Now we have an individual relationship and not a national relationship.

How much should we pay our pastor? What did Jesus say about profiting from ministry?

Matthew 21:12 And Jesus went into the temple of God, and cast out all that sold and bought in the temple, and overthrew the tables of the moneychangers, and the seats of them that sold doves. And said unto them, It is written my house shall be called a house of prayer; but you have made it a den of thieves. Overthrowing the businessmen was on the second of three consecutive days, Saturday Sunday, and Monday. The Saturday or Sabbath, He went to the temple as Priest. Sunday, the first day of the week. He went as King. The next day, Monday, the businessmen were gone, and He went to the temple as Prophet.

Today, we have people earning more in ministry than they

could earn in the real world. If the man could earn $40,000 a year as a mechanic and earns $60,000 as a minister, he has an economic incentive to serve Christ as a pastor. If he drives a car more expensive than his flock, he is certainly prospering in the ministry. Why should his church members believe anything he says, when he is so focused on material possessions. My uncle, Weldon Barnard was a pastor for almost 40 years in various small communities in Texas. He is the best example I know, of honoring this principle. He never prospered from serving Christ.

If Jesus came to your church, would he find them selling books and tapes? What is the difference between that and selling doves for sacrifices?

Did Jesus command us to help those less fortunate? Matthew 25:34-40 Then shall the king say unto them on his right hand, come you blessed of my father, inherit the kingdom prepared for you from the foundation of the world, for I was hungry and you gave me meat I was thirsty and you gave me drink I was a stranger and you took me in naked and you clothed me I was sick and you visited me I was in prison and you came unto me then shall the righteous answer him saying Lord when saw we you hungry and fed you or thirsty and gave you drink when saw we you a stranger and took you in or naked and clothed you or saw we you sick or in prison and came unto you and the king shall answer and say unto them verily I say unto you inasmuch as you have done it unto one of the least of my brethren you have done it unto me.

According to IRS statistics, the average American gives 1.56 percent of his income to charity including churches and religious organizations. Very few people are tithing. If they were, the church budgets would grow geometrically.

Luke 3:10-11. And the people asked him, saying. What shall we do then? he answered and said unto them, he that has two coats, let him impart to him that has none; and he that has meat, let him do likewise, living for self and not sharing with others. James 2:15-16 If a brother or sister be naked, and destitute of daily food, And one of you say unto them, Depart in peace, be you warmed and filled; notwithstanding you give them not those things with are needful to the body; what does it profit? It is the ultimate in hypocrisy to build a million dollar church building and allow Christians in the same city to go without food and clothing. Will God bless a church that so clearly violates his Word?

1 John 3:17-18 But whoever has this world's good, and sees his brother have need, and shuts up his bowels of compassion from him, how dwells the love of God in him?

Love is an action. Are poor people made to feel just as welcome in your church? My little children, let us not love in work, neither in tongue, but in deed and in truth.

Hebrews 13:16 But to do good and to communicate forget not, for with such sacrifices God is well pleased. Help those who cannot help themselves. Are those the people we want to help? Or do we want to help those who can help us someday?

Did Jesus evaluate the motive in giving? Mark 12:42-44 The widow and her two mites.

But he shall receive an hundred fold now in this time houses and brethren and sister and mothers and children and land with persecutions and in the world to come eternal life v31 But many that are first shall be last and the last first. We are going to be surprised in Heaven. Some blind poor grandmother who lived in the country is going to be first in line. On earth, they would not even drive her to church. But God is going to place her first in line. These famous and rich prosperity preachers on television, may find themselves last in line.

This is one of the most improperly used verses in Scripture. If God wanted to bless Christians with financial and material blessings, the entire world would be saved as soon as they heard of it. Isn't that what the five loaves and two fishes was all about? They followed Jesus across that the lake the next day because of the hope of material gain. For them Jesus was nothing more than a lottery ticket. No, Jesus would not fill his Heaven with greedy money hungry people. I suspect the only people who really profit from this garbage are the ones receiving the donations and contributions. Perhaps that is why they continue to preach the hundred fold philosophy. Unfortunately, there is no biblical basis for a Christian becoming wealthy. That would defeat the very message of salvation form sin, and a new life on the new earth with Christ.

Would Jesus expect us to tithe 100% in some cases? Luke 21:1-4 What about the widow and her two mites?

CHAPTER 11

AN EXAMPLE OF CHRISTIAN GIVING

2 Corinthians 8:1-6 is a verse that might relate to bake sales and car washes. What a puny weak God some churches serve. If they do not bake a cake and sell it for 50 cents, God cannot send the youth on a mission trip. Please, explain that philosophy. If God is so poor that he needs a rummage sale to help him out then he is not worth serving. If the church leadership does not want to buy shirts for the baseball team, do not do an end run around that decision by circumventing with a seemingly innocent fund raising activity. The only fund raising there should be in Church are the tithes and offerings coming voluntarily.

Paul did not ask for financial help. "Why are we better than Paul, and feel we should beg people to contribute? It must be a choice or a decision. It is between God and the giver. In fact, I recommend that gifts are in cash. Your pastor and elders and deacons should never know how much you give. The temptation is to give to impress them, or be in ear of what they would say. Remember, we lose our blessing if we give for the wrong reason.

What exhortation do we have for Christian giving?

2 Corinthians 8:7-15 next step in spiritual development. Tithers are not super Christians. Tithing is one of the baby steps in spiritual growth. Baby Christians are taught to tithe. Most of the edifying Scriptures are way beyond tithing. And we will cover those later.

What explanation do we have of Christian giving? 2 Corinthians 8:16-9:5 must report on how used.

What encouragement do we have for Christian giving? 2 Corinthians 9:6-13 blessed happiness.

I have met several very happy people. None of them were wealthy. 1 have never met a wealthy and happy person. I am sure there are some. I have read of them. But I would rather be happy than rich. Of course that is a convenient philosophy since I will never be wealthy.

What justification is there for paying preachers?

2 Corinthians 9:14 grace not law.

If someone in my church is poor, why should I help them? Romans 15:26 For it has pleased them of Macedonia and Achaia to make a certain contribution for the poor saints which are in Jerusalem, more than just material possessions to be shared.

Proverbs 25:21 If your enemy be hungry, give him bread to eat, and if he be thirsty, give him water to drink, For you shall heap coal of fire upon his head, and the Lord shall reward you. Jesus and Paul both repeat this proverb so it must be extremely important.

Why are other people doing better than me? Psalm 37:1. Fret not yourself because of evildoers.

Philippians 2:1-4 Look not every man on his own things but every man on the things of others. Are there any we should not help?

Philippians 3:2 Beware of dogs, beware of evil workers, beware of the concision. The people who comfort you are not telling you what you really need.

Colossians 3:8 But now you put off all these anger, wrath, malice, blasphemy, filthy communication out of your mouth

1 Timothy 5:8,13 But if any provide not for his own and especially for those of his own house he has denied the faith and is worse than an infidel. And with all they learn to be idle, wandering about from house to house and not only idle but tattlers also and busybodies, speaking things which they ought not.

What four groups of people we are not supposed to help with the money God has entrusted us with: 2 Thessalonians. 3:8- Neither did we eat any man's bread for nothing, but worked with labor and travail night and day, that we might not be chargeable to any of you. tentmaker until they could support him. We should be willing to do the same. Not because we have not power, but to make ourselves an example unto you to follow us. People say they are going to trust the Lord when what they really mean is they want to do something and hope the Lord rescues them. For even when we were with you, this we commanded you, that if any would not work, neither should he eat. This is routinely rejected by people in the church. However, it is very simple. You must have a job and an income. If you do not, you deserve nothing. God wants everyone to work. There is no Bible verse that excuses people from working. In fact, there are no vacations or retirements condoned in Scripture. God gives us one day a week to rest, spiritually, and He will sustain us otherwise.

2 Thessalonians. 3:14-15 If the person will not work, throw him out. He will only cause trouble. In the secular world if I have a troublemaker as an employee, I try to turn them around, if not possible, discharge them. To allow them to stay will hurt productivity and morale. It is far more serious in Church because the consequences of every action or decision affects eternity.

What am I thankful for? If you were thankful, you would thank God for every part of your body especially those parts that work normally. Feet, hands, arms, legs, pancreas, stomach, lungs, heart, eyes, ears, brains, etc. We would never have time to thank him. I heard an unknown speaker on the radio say, He spilled enough blood cells to allow for one cell for each person who will ever live. One of those had your name on it. He has the hairs of your head numbered. Your tears are in his bottle, according to the psalmist David. Your fingerprints, voice print, and DNA are unique.

Tithing is a part of worship.

CHAPTER 12

DAILY ESSENTIALS

The first priority was to God and his shepherd. The second priority is to survive today. Does this include spouse? children? parents? Have we made decisions which jeopardized daily essentials for our family? Has there been a time when the people depending upon us did not have what they needed, because of the consequences of our choice? Who is the ultimate provider? Who answers to God for the way in which basic needs of the family go unmet? What if we are not able to provide? What about the majority of the world, which goes to bed hungry?

Genesis 42:25 Joseph...gave them provision for way.

Genesis 45:11 And there nourish you...lest...poverty

Deuteronomy 15:11 For the poor shall never cease out of the land; therefore I command thee, saying, Thou shall open thine hand wide unto your brother, to the poor, and to the needy, in the land.

Joshua 9:5 Bread of provision dry and moldy

1 Kings 4:7 12 officers 1 each month provision King

Psalm 23:1 Lord is my shepherd, I shall not want

Psalm 68:19 Daily loads us with benefits

Psalm 123:15 Satisfy her poor with bread

Proverbs 10:15 Wealth strong city...destruction poor

Proverbs 11:24 That withholds more than meet, poverty.

Proverbs 20:13 Love not sleep lest come poverty

Proverbs 22:9 Bountiful eye blessed, gives poor.

Proverbs 23:31 Look not upon the wine when it is red.

Proverbs 24:30 I went by the field of the slothful, and by the vineyard of the man void of understanding. And lo, it was all grown over with nettles, and thorns had covered the face thereof and the stone wall was broken down. And considered. A little more sleep, a little more slumber, a little folding of the hands to rest, and your poverty shall break in upon you as an armed man, want as one...travels.

Proverbs 31:7 Let him drink and forget his poverty.

There are four groups of people we are not supposed to help with the money God has entrusted us with:

2 Thess. 3:10-11 Lazy. What if the lazy are ours?

2 Thess. 3:14-15 Sluggards. Same question?

Proverbs 28:22 Get rich quick schemes.

2 Cor. 8:13 Someone who wants the easy way.

This is going to be a problem for some people who feel as a Christian, that they must help anyone who asks.

To provide for our spouse, children, parents, and anyone living in our household. Then the poor as long as they are not the four groups above:

Exodus 20:12 Care for father and mother

Matthew 5:42 Give to him who asks of you

Matthew 10:42 Cup of water in my name

CHAPTER 13

HOW TO PROVIDE FOOD AND CLOTHING

Very little or no debt should routinely be employed in providing for food and clothing, or any personal need or want. Debt can be used for business purposes, and we shall see that in the next chapter, number 3.

No more than 5 percent of your gross income should be used to provide for food for your family. Food excludes entertainment. Eating at home is in the food budget. Eating away from home is in the Entertainment budget. The first priority was to God and his shepherd. The second priority is to survive today. Does this include spouse? children? parents? No more than 5 percent of your gross income should be used to provide for clothing for your family. Shoes are included in this category.

Some people use envelopes, the minimum wage is $5.15, but most adults are earning more than the minimum wage. If we use $10 per hour, that is approximately $20,800 per year. Since most families have both spouses working, that is $41,600 per year. Let's say your weekly gross earnings are $750. Five percent, or $150 is cashed and goes into the food envelope. That is what we can spend at the grocery store. We are going to pay cash so we cannot go over. If you go over you can use American Express for the difference or put something back. To avoid the embarrassment of going over, you will tend to be under. If you go under that money stays in the food envelope until next week and next week you have a little more than $150 to spend.

Clothing envelope is maintained in the same manner. Of course, if you cannot store cash safely in envelopes, it can be done conceptually, on a piece of paper, in concert with the checkbook. A shopping list must also be used with clothing. There are some differences with regard to clothing. First, try the "72 hour" rule. if it is a good deal, in terms of color, price, fit, etc., it still will be three days later. Utilizing this rule should cut your clothing expenditures in half. Much shopping for clothing is done at a shopping mall. There are several reasons why this is an undesirable financial strategy. First, we are placing in our vision thousands of things which we did not know we wanted. Jesus said pluck the eye out if it offends you. He was referring to the lust of a man, in his heart, when the man looked upon a woman God did not prepare for him. What is the difference for a woman or child when they go window shopping? This is not harmless Christian entertainment. When I see my friends at the mall, I ask them why they are there. I know my wife and I have a purpose in being there. So many say for entertainment. I beg to differ with that philosophy.

The lust of the eyes, the lust of the flesh, and the pride of life are no more present anywhere than at the shopping mall. Women do not dress appropriately at the mall. Men visit the mall because the women are there. Almost none knows exactly why they are there. And almost none are living within their means. We should not shop for clothes once a week. We should accumulate our clothing budget until Dad has a job interview, our son needs a new pair of shoes, Mom needs a dress for work (not church), and our daughters need school clothes. What about Proverbs 31. Lucky is the family who has someone who can sew. Also, fortunate is the woman who knows when to shop. How many times have you seen an article of clothing on sale for less than you paid for it? Study and effort in this department will be greatly rewarded.

Have we made decisions which jeopardized daily essentials for our family? Has there been a time when the people depending upon us did not have what they needed, because of the consequences of our choice?

Who is the ultimate provider?

Who answers to God for the way in which basic needs of the family are not met?

What if we are not able to provide?

What about the majority of the world, which goes to bed hungry?

Is God interested in our provision?

How did God use the circumstances of Joseph's family regarding food? Genesis 42:25 Then Joseph commanded to fill their sacks with corn, and to restore every man's money in to his sack, and to give them provision for the way, and thus did he unto them. God is concerned about your having food to eat. If you starve to death, who is going to tell the world about Jesus. Over 30,000 people in the world starve to death every day. Some of this number are surely believers. Yet, God has provided enough food to feed everybody. And enough ships and workers to get the food there. Why are they starving? Not because God lets it happen. Because sin is in the world. Greedy dictators rob their nations while their people starve. Is that the fault of God? Wars and strife interrupt the work and flow of raising and distributing food. Are the wars a fault of God? Why doesn't God stop it? Which sins should He intervene with? He has made provision for all sin by sending his son to die on the cross. During the 1,000 year reign on earth, there is no starvation and no wars. Not a single person will die from hunger during that thousand years. What is the difference? Same earth. Same human race. Same food. But Jesus rules.

Genesis 45:11 And there I will nourish you for yet there are five years of famine lest you and your household and all that you have come to poverty.

So many people ask when they should help and how they should help others. If following a Biblical pattern, you help with food. If my uncle is hungry, he can eat free at my house. If the same man needs a car or a computer or a lawn mower, he can still eat free at my house. We make things complicated because we don't want to utilize the Bible as our guidebook.

What did God command regarding the poor? Deuteronomy 15:11. Open wide your hand.

John 12:8 For the poor you will always have with you.

How do you resolve Deuteronomy 15:11 with John 12;8? If you want to help the poor, you have ample opportunity. If every church in America, spent an equal amount on the poor that they spend on their building, none would be hungry in this country. More people would hear the gospel as a result. It is not the building that draws people. Jesus said If I be lifted up I will draw all men unto me. Feeding the poor would lead to more of the gospel being preached. With more of the Gospel preached, more would be saved. Bottom line: Fewer people are saved because too much money is spent on church buildings. The cost of the carpeting alone in the churches in your town could feed the hungry. Is this really about human competition. I know of a church that purchased real gold for a dome atop their building. I assure not a single soul will come to Christ because of that gold dome. Could they at least refer to Jesus on their sign that changes each week?

Does God know the human heart? Will you encounter liars in this life?

Joshua 9:5 Gibeonites wore old shoes and old clothing. The Israelites were so gullible. We should be closer to the Holy Spirit and would not be so easily deceived.

How do you overcome the world? How do you overcome the flesh?

Ephesians 6:11,12 Put on the whole armor of God that you may be able to stand against the wiles of the devil. For we wrestle not against flesh and blood but against powers and principalities against powers against the rulers of the darkness of this world against spiritual wickedness in high places.

2 Corinthians 2:11 Lest Satan gets an advantage of us for we are not ignorant of his devices. What ever happened to confessing our sin, and repentance?

James 4:7 Submit yourselves therefore to God resist the devil and he will flee from you.

Is it possible that lies are communicated to you in the mail, and on mass media advertising?

What about taxation?

1 Kings 4:7 12 tribes 12 officers for food and clothing

Why is everything divided into 12 tribes?

What did our Lord Jesus Christ do when he returned to heaven after His death?

Are you part of this plan?

Can God see your future?

Can God be trusted with your future?

Psalm 132:151 will abundantly bless her provision I will satisfy her poor with bread.

What role do we play in His provision?

Proverbs 30:8 Neither poverty nor riches. Can the reader name one handicap which is difficult to overcome?

Does God trust us with extreme situations?

How do you provide for our spouse, children, parents, and anyone living in our household?

Does one of the ten commandments relate here? Exodus 20:12 honor your father and mother What about the second coming? What will happen when he comes?

Matthew. 24:45-46 good man of the house watching for the thief faithful and wise servant meat in his due season

Why do some have more?

John 9:4 I must work the works of Him that sent me while it is day.

Is there a relationship between the suffering of man and the glory of God?

What material possession is more valuable than Christ dying for the sins of all?

How can some give when they have so little? 2 Corinthians. 8:2 deep poverty abounded unto their liberality, poorest church gave the most.

For what reason are we created?

Ephesians 2:10 for we are his workmanship created in Christ Jesus for good works if you are rich none will come to Christ. What testimony do you have? They are blinded. What if we fail to provide for our family?

1 Timothy 5:8 worse than an infidel

Widows? 1 Timothy 5:16 take care of your own widows and not burdened the church is last resort.

How can we be in the world but not of it?

James 1:27 Pure religion and undefiled before God and the father is this, To visit the fatherless and widows in their affliction, and to keep himself unspotted from the world. We should know who is. once identified, we should be part of their solution. The government can feed them and provide them housing utilities transportation and health care. The government cannot tell them of a God who loves them.

How will men know that you are his disciple?

John 13:34-35 A new commandment I give unto you, That you love one another, as I have loved you that you also love one another. By this shall all men know that you are my disciples, if you have love one to another.

Romans 13:8. Owe no man any thing but to love one another. for he that loves another has fulfilled the law. I do not see much love today.

James 2:15-16 if a brother or sister be naked and destitute of daily food. praying for each other is not sufficient.

What about testing fruit?

How does love translate into action?

1 John 3:17-18 But who has this world's goods, and sees his brother have need, and shuts up his bowels of compassion from him, how dwells the love of God in him? To feed someone holding up a sign, and not tell him about Jesus, misses the whole point.

Where is your support?

3 John 5-6 beloved you do faithfully whatever you do to the brethren and to strangers. Which have borne witness of your charity before the church, whom if you bring forward on their

journey after a godly sort, you shall do well. Helping a person who is a false teacher, makes you their partner in crime.

What about hoarding food? What about the manna God provided to the Israelites?

What is so special about the 24 hour divisions of time? Why is God asking us to focus our plans this way?

The World is full of starving children. How can God allow it? What about the 1,000 year reign?

When shopping at the grocery store: remember a few simple guidelines:

1) Never shop when hungry or tired or stressed out;

2) Never shop when the store is busy;

3) Never take children to the store; or if necessary, find a path in the center of each aisle.

4) Use the same path each time. For instance, skip aisles and sections.

5) Always use a list, and stay close to it. Seventy percent of purchases at the grocery store are impulse items. In other words,

6) Never shop together;

7) Never purchase more than the menu for one week ahead.

8) Never buy more than the freezer, refrigerator or pantry can hold.

9) Never buy anything in order to win something free. For instance buy four pots and pans and get one free; and,

10) Purchase groceries with the concept that we are going to eat at home except on special occasions. And we are going to carry our lunch to work. Children's meals at school are different. Since their meals are subsidized with tax dollars, the school lunch is cheaper than you can send one to school. That is not the same for adult meals. You are going to average $7 per day, or $1,750, plus gas, and wear and tear on the vehicle to eat out. You can carry a lunch to work for approximately $3.00

per day. This saves approximately $1,000.00 a year just on lunch. By not eating out, the average American family saves $20.00 per week or $5,000 per year.

To eat out, is expensive and risky. There is no restaurant in the world as clean as your own kitchen. There is no restaurant in the world as safe as your own kitchen. There is no restaurant in the world as low in fat as your own kitchen. Why do we waste our money and risk our health and life?

People eat out for only three reasons: 1) Lust of the eyes; 2) Lust of the flesh; and 3) Pride of life.

What are the essentials?

1 Timothy 6:8 And having food and clothing let us therewith be content.

CHAPTER 14

BUILD YOUR BUSINESS

Did Adam have work to do, before the curse of tilling the land by the sweat of his brow? Do you consider the classification of every living creature work? Was the curse related to the frustration and inconsistency of results? What does it mean to build your business before you build your house in Proverbs 24:27? What is the biblical pattern for earning money?

How is prosperity achieved? Is there any biblical pattern other than diligence and integrity? Is there a set of guidelines for your career, job, or business? What does the Bible say about success in business? Can you be a good Christian, and make a profit? Is there a Bible verse that says something negative about work? The closest ones would be those that say not to neglect spiritual things and family needs.

Does God want you to succeed? How does God measure success? Is there anything material or physical that God will not sacrifice for your spiritual benefit? Does God feel your relationship to Him is important? Is it more important than earthly success? Would God allow you to be wealthy if it cost your relationship to him? If another believer has more money than you, does that mean they are more obedient to God?

Locate book, chapter, and verse that says: "The heart of the king is like the rivers of water. He turns it wherever he will." What application does this verse have for your career? Could it be that no human being is standing in your way? Could it be that God is directing your path through obstacles you think were placed by other people?

How does marriage relate to managing money? If you were asked to rearrange in Biblical order: marriage, children, investment, career, college, apprenticeship, engagement, house hunting, etc., could you do so accurately? What if our children do not follow this pattern? Genesis 2:24. Therefore shall a man leave his father and mother and cleave unto his wife, and they shall be one flesh. We have it backwards. People today, fall in love, get married, buy a house, and then go to college or look for a job. It should be college, job, house, and then marriage. Young couples want what mom and dad have. They ignore the fact that mom and dad worked and saved for 40 years to get to that level.

If you are a young man, and want to follow a Biblical pattern, try the following. By age thirteen, you should have an indication of your interests, skills, talents, gifts, abilities, and aptitude. Why thirteen? A Jewish boy became a man at his Bar mitzvah. This meant more than assuming a role in the synagogue. It meant he assumed a significant role in the family business. He worked for probably 10 years, but his real training began then. In modem day America, men usually work for a corporation, and therefore there is no opportunity for this. However, one can accomplish the next best thing.

Proverbs 22:6 requires a Christian man to do the same thing for each of his sons. By 13, each son should have had sufficient experience to know which direction they will head. If they are gifted academically, they would be in honors classes by this time. Or it may be called gifted and talented in your school district. During high school, a young man should know whether he is in the distributive education, ROTC, football, drama, building trades, automotive mechanics, etc. If not, Dad must help. Every year invested in the wrong path, is a year lost in that career.

By the time I was 14, I was discussing business with adults. I do not claim that I impressed them. However, their conversations were certainly longer than merely humoring an interested teenager. In the junior year of high school, I took a bookkeeping course. And I earned an outstanding achievement on the high school orientation examination, given annually by the Texas Society of Certified Public Accountants. By 16, I was ordering paint, supplies, and other merchandise for a retail paint store in Piano, TX. When I began college in 1973, my first, last, and only major was Accounting. High school was completed a semester early, and graduated with Honors. College was completed a semester early, and graduated with Honors. No course was ever attempted by error. Later in life, as a college professor I was frustrated with lost credits by students, every time a student changes majors or schools, they lose time, money, and effort. God has a plan which is efficient.

Let us return to the life cycle illustration. A Hebrew man had a business or career and a house, before his parents ever arranged his marriage. I realize no man today will allow that to happen. However, if parents arranged marriages, our nation would not have a fifty percent divorce rate. It would be so much improved. Our mothers especially, can tell a Proverbs 31 woman from the rest. Samson, David, and Solomon could not tell the difference. And I do not believe men today can either. Selection of a wife is in part a financial decision. If you select the wrong wife, it may end in divorce. If it ends in divorce, you will have an estate no better than half of what it would be otherwise. A divorce usually costs a million dollars. How? Take the money you lose in property settlements, child support payments, duplicate house and utility costs, and duplicate entertainment, and add that up. If that were saved and invested, what would it earn? At least one million for the average family. Does God care if you prosper? Maybe not. Does God care if you are divorced? Yes. Indirectly, you also save that money. We will speak more on housing in section five.

Does God really care about our work? Genesis 31:42 Except the God of my father, the God of Abraham, and the ear of Isaac, had been with me, surely you have sent me away now empty. God has seen mine affliction and the labor of my hand, and rebuked you in the past. Does God know when we have a bad day at work? Does He care? This verse and others, indicates that he does. He counted the years they were in bondage. Why would God count the years if he was not intimately aware of their struggle.

Can God prosper you in the presence of your enemies? Genesis 47:27 And Israel dwelt in the land of Egypt, in the country of Goshen, and had possessions therein, and grew, and multiplied exceedingly. What did the psalmist say in Psalm 23. THOU prepared a table before me in the presence of my enemies. When I worked for the City of Dallas, my supervisor wanted to give my job, to one of his friends, who happened to be my subordinate. They made a sustained effort to make me miserable enough to quit. Finally, after three and one-half years, they abolished my position so that I would be laid off. It was the only way to make me leave. During that difficult period, I earned two awards from the City of Dallas, taught courses for a Christian university part-time, completed many speaking engagements, and otherwise prospered. It does not matter who is against you if you are on the Lord's side.

Is it old fashioned not to work on Sunday? Where in the new Testament was this prohibition eliminated. The Ten Commandments have never been dropped. However, on rare occasions I have. I did not ask forgiveness even though I was criticized by other believers. I believe in the Sabbath, and I believe it is for my benefit, as Jesus said. If your job requires Sunday work such as the military, nursing, convenience store, computer reservations, etc., fulfill the obligation you made to your employer, if you cannot transfer or promote out of Sunday, then I believe God wants you to search for a job that does not require it. A nurse can change from a hospital to a doctor's office. I believe that God will honor the move. And I believe the pay cut will be rewarded in many other ways, ways you do not realize.

One of the occasions I voluntarily took a cut in pay, was to accept a teaching position at Christian university. It was a financial hardship but one I have never regretted. During my two years there, I had the opportunity to adopt a newborn baby boy, whom we named Sterling. My lifelong dream of fatherhood would not have been fulfilled had I not followed the Lord's will two years before.

Does God evaluate our performance at work? II Chronicles 19:6 You judge not for man, but for the Lord. Why do bad and lazy people get paid more than us? Psalm 37:1-7

Fret not thyself because of evildoers

Proverbs 11:1 A false balance is abomination to the Lord, but a just weight is his delight.

There are many ways to get ahead in life. Lying, cheating, deceiving, stealing, intimidating, destroying, and other evil methods are certainly successful. However, there is a way to succeed and do so in a way that honors the Lord.

Here are several verses to guide you on that point. Do we earn our promotions?

Psalm 75:6 Promotion comes not from the East or west, nor from the south.

Psalm 101:7 He that works deceit shall not dwell in my house he that tells lies shall not tarry in my sight.

Psalm 127:1 Except the Lord build the house they labor in vain that build it. Except the Lord keep the city the watchman wakes but in vain. It is vain for you to rise up early, to sit up late, and to eat the bread of sorrows, for so he gives his beloved sleep.

Proverbs 3:35 The wise shall inherit glory but shame shall be the promotion of fools.

God judges rich people. Why are they held to a higher standard. It is within their power to help people. And who gave them the power? Why did God give it to them. You may be in a hurry to be rich. However, more will be expected of you by the Lord.

Proverbs 10:5 He that gathers in summer is a wise son but he that sleeps in harvest is a son that causes shame.

Proverbs 6:6-10 The first one of these suggests we Consider the ant. The second suggests how sleep should be viewed. I believe these verses indicate the following. If you are a Christian, you should be the first one at the office, shop, or factory every morning. You should have the coffee brewing by the time they drag in. You should have the best attendance record. And you should do more in four hours, than an unbeliever does in a day. You should have the best attitude. I have fired Christians for a variety of reasons. Some of them brought their bibles, and witnessed. Of course, I did not fire them for that. I fired them because they were bad employees, and repeated efforts at counseling were to no avail. Will God bless you if you are a bad employee? Obviously, not. If merely being a Christian guaranteed the blessings of God, we would not need most of the new testament.

What about shortcuts to success?

Proverbs 1:17 surely in vain the net is spread in the sight of any bird

Proverbs 1:19 so are the ways of everyone that is greedy of gain, which takes away the life of the owners thereof.

Proverbs 3:9-10 Honor the lord with your substance and with the first fruits of all your increase. So shall your barns be filled with plenty, and your presses shall burst out with new wine. If your checkbook was published what would other believers say? God sees it already.

How should we feel about those lower in our organization? Proverbs 3:27 Withhold not good to whom it is due,

when it is in the power of thine your hand to do it.

When I worked at the City of Dallas, a fellow supervisor advised me not to be friendly with the cleaning crew. He felt we were above that. My response was that God made us all, and talking to them did not diminish my rank and authority.

When should we sign our name to a contract?

Proverbs 6:1 My son if you be surety for your friend, if you have stricken your hand with a stranger. THOU are snared with the words of your mouth, you are taken with the words of your mouth.

Proverbs 11:15 He that is surety for a stranger shall smart for it and he that hates suretyship is sure. When should we sign for the debts of another? never. When someone asks you for this help, tell them the Bible says no. Show them the two verses above. Show them this book. Offer to help them in many other ways. There is no prohibition against your verbal intervention in their behalf. But have you considered, that obstacle is God's way of telling them no. Then you are going to come along and overrule God. God will teach you both a lesson.

Will every Christian be rich? it is unlikely that even a small percentage will be better off than the unbelievers. Proverbs 8:18 riches and honor are with me, yes durable riches and righteousness fruit is better than gold yes than fine gold and my revenue than choice silver. Will any true Christians be rich in material terms?

Proverbs 10:4 he becomes poor that deals with a slack hand, but the hand of the diligent makes rich.

Proverbs 11:4 riches profit not in the day of wrath but righteousness delivers from death.

Who should you ask? When people are considering a divorce they ask a divorced person. What logic is that? Ask a married person about divorce. When people are contemplating a financial decision, ask a financial person. Surely someone in your church has achieved some type of licensure or certification by secular standards. If they know some of the Bible, they can be even a bigger help. If there is no person available, call us. It is free, and we do not solicit. Although we will accept if offered. One thing we cannot do is discuss specific investments. And no person in your church can either unless they have a Securities license. More on finding a counselor in the investments discussion.

Proverbs 11:14 Where no counsel is the people fall but in the multitude of counselors there is safety

Proverbs 11:16 A gracious woman retains honor, and strong men retain riches.

What about Ruth? Who says women do not know about business. Women are better than men, when it comes to budgeting. Every family or married couple I ever counseled, it turned out the man was to blame for the debt. Your wife is the best business advisor you will ever have. She will help you more than I can. Listen to her. You do not have to follow all of the advice, but listen.

Employee relations. You should be the best employer in town. Almost invariably, when an employee leaves us, they call within one year wanting their old job back. Proverbs 12:10-11 Righteous man regards the life of his beast, but the tender mercies of the wicked are cruel. Proverbs 12:24 The hand of the diligent bear rule but the slothful shall be under tribute.

The following verses have one phrase listed. What does the entire verse mean to you?

Proverbs 13:11 Wealth gotten by vanity.

Proverbs 13:18 Poverty shame to refuse instruction.

Proverbs 13:20 He that walks wise men shall be wise.

Proverbs 13:22 A good man leaves an inheritance.

Proverbs 13:23 Much food is in the tillage of the poor.

I think they reinforce the previous discussions with the concept that your work life is no different from your spiritual life. To the Jews, work is a form of prayer.

Proverbs 14:4 Where no oxen are, the crib is clean but much increase is by the strength of the ox.

If you have a problem we want to get rid of the ox. We throw out the troublemaker at work and in our church. We want to avoid cleaning the crib but we are better off in the long run by taking care of the problem.

Here are additional proverbs to guide you at work. They have helped me and I hope they will help you. For the sake of brevity, have paraphrased the highlights.

Proverbs 15:6 In the house of the righteous is much treasure but in the revenues of the wicked is trouble.

Proverbs 17:5 Who mocks poor reproaches maker.

Proverbs 17:18 Void of understanding strikes hands.

Proverbs 18:9 Slothful man brother to great waster.

Proverbs 18:4 Words of man's mouth as great waters.

Proverbs 19:1 Better poor that walks in his integrity.

Proverbs 19:14 House and riches inheritance of father.

Proverbs 19:15 Slothfulness casts into a deep sleep.

Proverbs 19:20 Hear counsel, receive instruction.

Proverbs 19:24 Slothful man hides his hand in bosom.

Proverbs 27:6 Faithful are the wounds of a friend; but the kisses of an enemy are deceitful.

7The full soul loatheth an honeycomb; but to the hungry soul every bitter thing is sweet.

8 As a bird that wandereth from her nest, so is a man that wandereth from his place.

9 Ointment and perfume rejoice the heart: so doth the sweetness of a man's friend by hearty counsel.

A prudent man foreseeth the evil, and hideth himself; but the simple pass on, and is punished. Proverbs 27:2

There are a few mistakes to avoid. Some of these are very popular. One should never borrow against a retirement account or use home equity. Borrowing against a retirement account is the same thing as trading your retirement years for some apparent need today. As for borrowing against home equity, we might ask people who lost their homes as a result. Is there any need worth your house? If a family member needed surgery and the health insurance was insufficient, a retirement account or a house pales in comparison. But I can think of very few situations where borrowing against a retirement account or home equity, could be justified.

With regard to credit card debt and the previous discussion, I still do not recommend it. When I fashion a get out of debt plan for someone, I leave retirement accounts and the home equity alone. The argument in favor is that I can exchange a higher rate of interest on the credit card for a lower rate of interest on this type of borrowing. Exchanging debt for debt makes sense with a 30 year first mortgage. Otherwise, it does not make sense because it is full of sound and fury signifying nothing. Excessive debt and the wrong type of debt are much more serious problems than the rate of interest one pays.

Another reason not to borrow on retirement accounts is income taxes. We pay taxes on the money we use to repay a loan against a retirement account. Think about the fact that we are paying taxes twice on the same dollar. One of the benefits of a retirement account is the tax advantages. By borrowing against a retirement account, we have just eliminated some of the tax advantages.

13 Take his garment that is surety for a stranger, and take a pledge of him for a strange woman. Proverbs 27:12 Proverbs 27:13

Whoso keepeth the fig tree shall eat the fruit thereof: so he that waiteth on his master shall be honoured.

19 As in water face answereth to face, so the heart of man to man.

20 Hell and destruction are never full; so the eyes of man are never satisfied.

21 As the fining pot for silver, and the furnace for gold; so is a man to his praise.

22 Though thou shouldest bray a fool in a mortar among wheat with a pestle, yet will not his foolishness depart from him.

23 Be thou diligent to know the state of thy flocks, and look well to thy herds.

24 For riches are not for ever: and doth the crown endure to every generation?

25 The hay appeareth, and the tender grass sheweth itself, and herbs of the mountains are gathered.

26 The lambs are for thy clothing, and the goats are the price of the field.

27 And thou shalt have goats' milk enough for thy food, for the food of thy household, and for the maintenance for thy maidens. Proverbs 27:17 Proverbs 27:18 Proverbs 27:19 Proverbs 27:20 Proverbs 27:23 Proverbs 27:24 Proverbs 27:26 Proverbs 27:27

The wicked flee when no man pursueth: but the righteous are bold as a lion.

2 For the transgression of a land many are the princes thereof: but by a man of understanding and knowledge the state thereof shall be prolonged.

3 A poor man that oppresseth the poor is like a sweeping rain which leaveth no food.

4 They that forsake the law praise the wicked: but such as keep the law contend with them.

5 Evil men understand not judgment: but they that seek the LORD understand all things.

6 Better is the poor that walketh in his uprightness, than he that is perverse in his ways, though he be rich.

7 Whoso keepeth the law is a wise son: but he that is a companion of riotous men shameth his father.

8 He that by usury and unjust gain increaseth his substance, he shall gather it for him that will pity the poor.

9 He that turneth away his ear from hearing the law, even his prayer shall be abomination.

10 Whoso causeth the righteous to go astray in an evil way, he shall fall himself into his own pit: but the upright shall have good things in possession.

11 The rich man is wise in his own conceit; but the poor that hath understanding searcheth him out.

12 When righteous men do rejoice, there is great glory: but when the wicked rise, a man is hidden.

13 He that covereth his sins shall not prosper: but whoso confesseth and forsaketh them shall have mercy.

14 Happy is the man that feareth alway: but he that hardeneth his heart shall fall into mischief.

15 As a roaring lion, and a raging bear; so is a wicked ruler over the poor people.

16 The prince that wanteth understanding is also a great oppressor: but he that hateth covetousness shall prolong his days.

17 A man that doeth violence to the blood of any person shall flee to the pit; let no man stay him.

18 Whoso walketh uprightly shall be saved: but he that is perverse in his ways shall fall at once.

19 He that tilleth his land shall have plenty of bread: but he that followeth after vain persons shall have poverty enough.

20 A faithful man shall abound with blessings: but he that maketh haste to be rich shall not be innocent.

21 To have respect of persons is not good: for a piece of bread that man will transgress.

22 He that hasteth to be rich hath an evil eye, and considereth not that poverty shall come upon him.

23 He that rebuketh a man afterwards shall find more favour than he that flattereth with the tongue.

24 Whoso robbeth his father or his mother, and saith, It is no transgression; the same is the companion of a destroyer.

25 He that is of a proud heart stirreth up strife: but he that putteth his trust in the LORD shall be made fat.

26 He that trusteth in his own heart is a fool: but whoso walketh wisely, he shall be delivered.

27 He that giveth unto the poor shall not lack: but he that hideth his eyes shall have many a curse. Proverbs 28:1 Proverbs 28:6 Proverbs 28:8 Proverbs 28:11 Proverbs 28:16 Proverbs 28:19 Proverbs 28:20 Proverbs 28:21 Proverbs 28:22 Proverbs 28:24 Proverbs 28:25 Proverbs 28:26 Proverbs 28:27

The king that faithfully judgeth the poor, his throne shall be established for ever. Proverbs 29:14

A man's pride shall bring him low: but honour shall uphold the humble in spirit. Proverbs 29:23

Many seek the ruler's favour; but every man's judgment cometh from the LORD.

Proverbs 29:26

Remove far from me vanity and lies: give me neither poverty nor riches; feed me with food convenient for me Proverbs 30:8

1 The words of king Lemuel, the prophecy that his mother taught him.

2 What, my son? and what, the son of my womb? and what, the son of my vows?

3 Give not thy strength unto women, nor thy ways to that which destroyeth kings.

4 It is not for kings, O Lemuel, it is not for kings to drink wine; nor for prince's strong drink:

5 Lest they drink, and forget the law, and pervert the judgment of any of the afflicted.

6 Give strong drink unto him that is ready to perish, and wine unto those that be of heavy hearts.

7 Let him drink, and forget his poverty, and remember his misery no more.

8 Open thy mouth for the dumb in the cause of all such as are appointed to destruction.

9 Open thy mouth, judge righteously, and plead the cause of the poor and needy.

10 Who can find a virtuous woman? for her price is far above rubies.

11 The heart of her husband doth safely trust in her, so that he shall have no need of spoil.

12 She will do him good and not evil all the days of her life.

13 She seeketh wool, and flax, and worketh willingly with her hands.

14 She is like the merchants' ships; she bringeth her food from afar.

15 She riseth also while it is yet night, and giveth meat to her household, and a portion to her maidens.

16 She considereth a field, and buyeth it: with the fruit of her hands she planteth a vineyard.

17 She girdeth her loins with strength, and strengtheneth her arms.

18 She perceiveth that her merchandise is good: her candle goeth not out by night.

19 She layeth her hands to the spindle, and her hands hold the distaff.

20 She stretcheth out her hand to the poor; yea, she reacheth forth her hands to the needy.

21 She is not afraid of the snow for her household: for all her household are clothed with scarlet.

22 She maketh herself coverings of tapestry; her clothing is silk and purple.

23 Her husband is known in the gates, when he sitteth among the elders of the land.

24 She maketh fine linen, and selleth it; and delivereth girdles unto the merchant.

25 Strength and honour are her clothing; and she shall rejoice in time to come.

26 She openeth her mouth with wisdom; and in her tongue is the law of kindness.

27 She looketh well to the ways of her household, and eateth not the bread of idleness.

28 Her children arise up, and call her blessed; her husband also, and he praiseth her.

29 Many daughters have done virtuously, but thou excellest them all.

30 Favour is deceitful, and beauty is vain: but a woman that feareth the LORD, she shall be praised.

31 Give her of the fruit of her hands; and let her own works praise her in the gates.

Proverbs 31 For at least two years before meeting my wife. I prayed for a Proverbs 31 wife. Then when I met her for the first time, only her mother was still alive, her father had died several years before. I asked her mother for permission before I ever asked my wife.

Write your plan to find a wife, if single. Write your plan to train your children if you have one or more. Or, if single and no children or children already married, write your plan to help those in your church. Regardless, write your plan to develop your career or business. 10 percent of your gross salary should be reinvested in this category (see budget example).

In later chapters we will develop the strategy to Pay yourself first. And we will consider investing as well. We will consider building your income stream before you spend it. It is easy to spend money. Is more difficult to save money.

CHAPTER 15

TRANSPORTATION

Can the reader be successful without dependable transportation? Is your wife, mother, or daughter safe in the vehicle you provided for them? What car should I drive? How much can I afford? What is the motivation for selecting the car I drive?

Related references:

Riches and honour are with me; yea, durable riches and righteousness.

Proverbs 8:18;

A man's heart deviseth his way: but the LORD directeth his steps. Proverbs 16:9;

He that loveth pleasure shall be a poor man: he that loveth wine and oil shall not be rich. Proverbs 21:17;

Labour not to be rich: cease from thine own wisdom. Proverbs 23:4;

Wilt thou set thine eyes upon that which is not? for riches certainly make themselves wings; they fly away as an eagle toward heaven. Proverbs 23:5

Give to him that asketh thee, and from him that would borrow of thee turn not thou away. Matthew 5:42

For this ye know, that no whoremonger, nor unclean person, nor covetous man, who is an idolater, hath any inheritance in the kingdom of Christ and of God. Ephesians 5:5

Ye ask, and receive not, because ye ask amiss, that ye may consume it upon your lusts. James 4:3

Whose adorning let it not be that outward adorning of plaiting the hair, and of wearing of gold, or of putting on of apparel;

4But let it be the hidden man of the heart, in that which is not corruptible, even the ornament of a meek and quiet spirit, which is in the sight of God of great price.

1 Peter 3:3-4

Expensive cars costly to insure and repair. Auto insurance essential elements not frills such as medical insurance and uninsured motorists (above state law). Pay in full not per month.

Comparison shopping should probably be a routine effort. This has become much easier online. Proverbs 31 makes reference to this practice and women seem to practice this more than men.

How to provide for Transportation

Can you be successful without dependable transportation? This chapter follows immediately after building your business, because it is the first thing you must have in order to earn money. What is the relationship between my work and transportation?

Debt is acceptable if the corporation or business owns or leases the vehicle, assuming the business can support that. There is no debt allowed for personal vehicles. No matter what your vehicles or their financing, the woman of the family gets the best car. That is part of provision. Is your wife, mother, or daughter safe in the vehicle you provided for them?

What car should I drive? You can drive any car you can pay cash for. How much can I afford? What is your savings account balance? Some purchase a car, truck, or van, because once a year, they take a vacation. This is a ridiculous strategy. Why pay thousands of dollars more for one or two weeks a year. I would never take one of the vehicles I owned on a trip or vacation. We rent, sometimes for as low as $200 per week. Each additional mile on your vehicle represents wear and tear that accelerates the demise and moves up the occasion that you must buy another car. This is also why taking a pleasure drive on Sunday afternoon is far more expensive than you realize. If you want to relax, take a walk. Taking a drive could be a $30 or $40 trip.

Matthew 5:42 Give to him that asks of you. Who is in your social circle that needs your help?

Proverbs 21:17 He that loves pleasure shall be poor. How much effort are you devoting to your own entertainment?

Proverbs 23:4   Labor not to be rich.

DO YOU WANT TO BE WEALTHY?

Proverbs 23:5 Riches have wings and fly. Have you heard of a rich person who lost it all?

Riches and honour are with me; yea, durable riches and righteousness. Proverbs 8:18

Riches and honor are with God. Do you know a rich person who is in love with God?

Proverbs 16:9 Man's heart devises. Lord directs. Has anything you planned ever worked out the way you thought it will?

In order to have an expensive car, can you justify how costly it is to purchase, insure, repair and maintain?

Have you reviewed your auto insurance policy descriptions of essential elements (not frills such as medical insurance and uninsured motorists (above state law))?

Have you considered whether or not to pay in full for six or twelve months, rather than on a per month basis? What about oil changes? It is cheaper in the short run, not to pay $30 for an oil change. However, in the long run, this investment extends the useful life of the vehicle, and therefore saves far more than the cost of the oil change. What about the three grades of fuel? It is cheaper in the short run, to purchase the least expensive gasoline.

However, in the long run, this investment extends the useful life of the vehicle, and therefore saves far more than the pennies per gallon difference in gasoline.

Did you comparison shop?

Forget about what others think. Forget about what you want. Realize your unbelieving neighbors are watching you.

And if you are a pastor, elder, or deacon, you should not have a car which far exceeds those of the people in your church. live within your means. This is the number one reason reported by self made millionaires. As soon as we purchased a new Honda Accord, we maintained saving at the same rate. Some people would relax and enjoy themselves. But a Christian life is one of discipline. I continued saving the first month, even though we had a brand new car in the driveway. Plan ahead. Stay with the plan. Watch God bless you when you attempt to provide for transportation needs using scriptural principles.

CHAPTER 16

Insurance and Medical care

Insurance and Medical care

Next, Health of myself, spouse, children, parents, etc. Do we know these things will happen? Does God expect us to prepare for things which are inevitable? Would God ask us to prepare for the rapture and for Heaven, but not prepare for the inevitable things on earth?

Proverbs 12:16 Prudent man covers shame.

Proverbs 13:16 Prudent man deals in knowledge.

Proverbs 16:21 Wise in heart shall be called prudent.
Proverbs 19:14 House and riches inheritance father.

Psalm 50:14-15 Call upon God in the day of trouble.

- Term life.
- Disability.
- Over 65 Long term care. We all agree this is nice to have. Is it a luxury or a necessity? Is it budgeted? By the time we realize we need it, it is very late in the process and therefore much more expensive.
- Longevity insurance (annuities)
- Renters insurance. The Bible says we should count the cost before making a decision. Therefore, no general statement can be made that would apply to all tenancy situations.

HOW TO PROVIDE FOR INSURANCE AND MEDICAL CARE

Key verse. The wise man foresees the evil and hides himself, but the simple passes on and is punished. Does God expect us to prepare for things which are inevitable? Would God ask us to prepare for the rapture and for Heaven, but not prepare for the inevitable things on earth? Knowing that we are growing old, would God alert us to the needs of old age? Jesus said to Peter, that when you are old someone will lead you by the hand and take you where you do not want to go. In the Old testament, the Bible refers to going out and coming in. A reference to being able to take care of business. If you cannot work when you are old or ill, does God want you to prepare for that?

In the Biblical economy, your children should provide for you. There is no scriptural basis for admitting your parents to a nursing home or residential center. However, I do not advise my clients to rely on the good nature of their children, even Christian children. If that happens, you have lost nothing by preparing otherwise. I recommend Medicare insurance as a place to start. Medicare pays approximately one-third of a physician charges. That makes you a less desirable patient for your physician. This dichotomy will exacerbate in this new millennium.

The next best solution is to be in a church that will help you the way the New Testament says to care for widows and orphans. God has put a nurse or someone like them in almost every church just for this purpose. It is the same way he puts a CPA, and an auto mechanic in each church.

The third best solution is to have a pile of cash. You should accumulate approximately $30,000 per person for this purpose. This should be in addition to your retirement and living expenses.

Here are some applicable verses:

Proverbs 12:16 Prudent man covers shame.

When you make the right decision you may not be noticed.

Proverbs 13:16 Prudent man deals in knowledge.

Knowledge and what Uncle Joe said, might be different. If I have an electrical repair, I call a licensed electrician. My electrician is named Jack and I would not consider using anyone else. If I have a telephone repair I call Ray. And so on. I always use licensed individuals. Hopefully, I get everything done right the first time, and to last. The most expensive decision is to pick the cheapest-pest alternative, The cheapest right now is the most expensive in the long run. A chain link fence is cheaper than a wooden one today. Two years later when you decide you really need a wooden one, you have then bought two fences when one would do. You can save $1 per month on car insurance by doubling your deductible from $250 to $500. If you have one claim in the next 20 years, it has cost you more money by saving the $1. The grocery store across town has cheaper eggs. Yet, the loss in value on your car plus the cost more than compensates for the apparent savings.

Proverbs 16:21 Wise in heart shall be called prudent.

Proverbs 19:14 House and riches inheritance father. Psalm 50:14-15 Call upon God in the day of trouble.

Who invented money? Who designed business? Is anybody a better business person than God?

Only if you think you will die someday. If the rapture is taking you and your entire family, and you know when it is going to happen, you would not need life insurance. However, since the Bible says no man knows the day or the hour, you need to purchase life insurance. Why is term life the best decision? It provides coverage when you need it and no additional time. Whole life and universal life provide coverage after your income ends. Therefore you are purchasing insurance to protect and income stream which no longer exists. That is why it is such rip-off. Another rip-off is life insurance for children. Why? What income stream are we protecting, my son is 16 and I do not depend on his income. My wife works part time but I do not depend on her income. No life insurance was purchased on either of their lives. On mine, yes. How much? Enough so my wife never has to worry about income.

What about health insurance. 39% of adult working Americans do not have health insurance. Many couples have told me they are trusting the Lord. This is the most worn out excuse

I have heard. These same couples drive to their appointment in a more expensive vehicle than I drive, the truth is that God has provided every individual, couple and family, enough to survive. We do not like what God provided us. We do not want to live within the boundaries God placed on us. We use the resources he gave us for items different than what he wanted. Then when there is not enough due to our choices, we say we are going to trust the Lord. How can God bless that?

In my business, I see Christian couples with no insurance seeking medical care. In many cases, they are receiving a level of medical care far below what others may receive. I formerly worked at Parkland hospital in Dallas. This institution delivers more babies than any facility in the free world. In an emergency they perform admirably. But I would not want my wife to sit and wait several hours for each prenatal appointment. If any man provide not for his own he is worse than an infidel. When I worked for an orthopedic surgery group, Medicaid would only pay for the old fashioned plaster white casts for children. The new high tech brightly colored Fiberglas casts cost three times as much ($70 back them). We gave them to all children regardless of who was on Medicaid. we felt that we would bear the loss so those children could have the same kind of casts. For my three broken arms, they had not yet invented the fiberglass cast.

DO I NEED DISABILITY INSURANCE?

Again, the family, first, the church second. After that, we have to ask what the chances are of us being unable to do our job or earn a living for several months. Of course, we should have a savings account for this purpose. Do I need an over 65 Long term care policy? Same answer. Should I consider Longevity insurance (annuities)? I recommend annuities as a method of maintaining income streams. How can we make sense of all of these important questions?

Is it necessary to purchase Renters' insurance? Twice my home has been hit by tornadoes, with me inside, once when I was 14 and again when I was 35. On each occasion, items were lost which were covered by typical homeowners insurance. If you are going to rent for an extended period of time, it is recommended.

God wants you to prepare for what you know is coming: death, retirement, disability, injury, illness, theft, vandalism, and catastrophe. Be prudent.

Proverbs Prepare thy work without, and make it fit for thyself in the field; and afterwards build thine house.

It is better to dwell in the corner of the housetop, than with a brawling woman and in a wide house. Proverbs 25:24

If an ox gore a man or a woman that they die: then the ox shall be surely stoned, and his flesh shall not be eaten; but the owner of the ox shall be quit. Exodus 21:28

5If any of you lack wisdom, let him ask of God, that giveth to all men liberally, and upbraideth not; and it shall be given him.

6But let him ask in faith, nothing wavering. For he that wavereth is like a wave of the sea driven with the wind and tossed.

7For let not that man think that he shall receive any thing of the Lord.

8A double minded man is unstable in all his ways.

James 1:5-8

CHAPTER 17

SHELTER

Housing, repairs, improvements, maintenance, utilities, mortgage payment.

Is it acceptable to borrow money for a house? What is the ideal arrangement? What happened to the inheritance practices of the old testament? Did God institute that, or was it man made? Where has God placed me on the income pyramid in society? Whose standard? How much? What percentage?

Proverbs 24:27   Prepare your work without, and make it first fit in the field.

- Buy second home first. The starter home concept is more a function of financing than it is a sound business practice. There are many hidden costs every time a house is sold or bought. This may or may not include improvements, furniture or furnishings which fit only one house. Then there are the financing costs associated with each transaction.

- Forced savings. Home ownership does force people to save funds by utilizing them for housing and housing related costs.

- Tax shelter. If one itemizes, a taxpayer can claim property taxes. In addition, the property taxes on a rental house can be claimed on Schedule E. Whether or not Schedule A or E is used, the property taxes can be claimed. Also, the appreciation on the house is usually not taxable.

- Not an investment. Buy only once. A house is an investment only if it is turned over. Anything purchased to use and keep is not an investment vehicle. An investment vehicle must have a return on investment. A house ROI could only be realized by no longer needing a house.
- Insurance. Homeowner's, Flood or earthquake, umbrella Liability. More is better where insurance is concerned. Any homeowner's insurance provider will probably offer a wide range of insurance products and services. Please do not ignore them. Although they are trying to sell you, it is worth listening to.

Reverse mortgage (AARP or Scholen or Buss). Homeowner receives money each month secured by equity. Die, bank sells house, pays costs, and keeps profit. Or give to church, tax deduction, church acts as a bank.

How To Provide For Shelter

What should I spend on housing, repairs, improvements, maintenance, utilities, mortgage payment, etc.? Is it acceptable to borrow money for a house? What is the ideal arrangement? What happened to the inheritance practices of the old testament? Did God institute that, or was it man made? Where has God placed me on the income pyramid in society? Whose standard? How much? What percentage? When? Proverbs 24:27 Build your business before you build your house. See chapter 3. How much of a payment can I handle? Proverbs 25:24 Comment on James 1:5-8 regarding a home mortgage. What does it mean to buy the second home first? Is a house, forced savings, a tax shelter, or an investment? An investment is only an investment if it is purchased for either an annual return or an eventual profit. A house is generally not considered an investment. It is however, one of the eight buckets that we are told to store our money in. We will see more of that when we consider investing in general in a later chapter.

What about homeowner's insurance? We have generally concluded that insurance is a Biblical use of money. Some types of insurance however are to be avoided and some are more important than others. Homeowners insurance is required by the mortgage company but is a good decision even if there is no mortgage.

What about reverse mortgages? A reverse mortgage allows a person to remain in their house as long as they live and also receive some monthly income. The amount depends upon whether there is any debt associated with the property, its value, age and the age of the owners. It is worth considering for the people who do not want to move out of the family homestead.

What is God's plan regarding housing. Few subjects are so clearly spelled out as this one is. The ideal choice if you are the oldest son is to inherit the house your parents are in. There are many reasons why this is not possible in our society. First, the greed of the parents. Second, the greed of the children. Third, the location of the career of the son.

I was born in Dallas, and resided in that area until graduating with my first degree. Then I worked in Washington dc, Virginia, San Antonio, Dallas, and now Wichita falls. My parents live in Justin which is three hours from me now.

If the oldest son was inappropriate as a recipient, the second son gets the house. Inappropriate was strictly interpreted as it was very unusual to pass over the eldest son. You may say we are not Hebrews in the old testament. I say yes. you are right. I do not invest in sheep, however, the financial principles came from God and not the Hebrews. And God is the same yesterday today and forever.

The second best way to provide for a house, is through the business. In times past, a store was purchased with living quarters above or on the side. This can still be done such as purchasing an apartment complex or motel. I owned a small building once. The rent from tenants paid more than the monthly mortgage payment. In some situations, police officers or maintenance men receive free rent form an apartment complex.

The third best way is to pay cash. Is this impossible? yes, if you want a house like other people have. At 12% compounded, $765.28 would be required to invest each month to accumulate $100,000. In some towns and counties, houses can be purchased for less than some people pay for cars.

What to you think about this excerpt from the best selling book, "The Millionaire Next Door", by Thomas Stanley and William Danko. The authors say that the typical wealthy individual is a businessman or woman who has lived in the same town for all of his adult life, and owns a small factory, or a chain of stores, or a service company. He lives next door to people with a fraction of this wealth. Their survey indicated that while the paycheck to paycheck crowd drives new cars, most millionaires do not. They are not wearing expensive clothes and watches and their houses are relatively modest compared to their financial status.

The fourth best way is a seven year mortgage. Why seven? Because no debt in the Bible was ever allowed to continue beyond seven years.

The fifth best way is a fifteen year mortgage.

The sixth best way is a 20-year mortgage. And the last of all the choices is the typical 30-year mortgage. God says we should fulfill our vows. Is it not a vow to sign a mortgage? God says we should not presume that God will act or anything will be a certain way in the future. Is not this the height of presumption, to sign a mortgage? You are obligating God since you are a believer. And yet God did not tell you to buy a house you cannot afford.

Of course, the difference between a 15 and 30 year mortgage on a $200,000 house at six percent is approximately $350 per month. Most people will not pay this much more and very few exercise this option.

What about the mortgage payment. No more than 25% of your gross salary including utilities. For most of you it is too late. However, the next time you purchase and finance, consider paying 20% or more on the down payment. This will eliminate the need to purchase the required mortgage insurance. Also, one might consider paying more up front in exchange for reducing the interest rate. There are almost no mortgage assumptions now but this is still a good way to go.

Try to arrange for housing with Scripture in mind.

CHAPTER 18

INCAPACITY AND DEATH, INCLUDING RETIREMENT

Preparation for the inevitable. Passage from this life to the next.

Increasing age and Retirement. Should I leave an inheritance to my children? Is there something more valuable than money that I could leave to them? Am I providing them with a temptation to want my demise? Was the old testament inheritance essentially a farm or ranch? Are we really talking about a way to survive? Is a career or an education closer to that than dollars?

Proverbs 19:14 House and riches inheritance of father
Ecclesiastes 5:19-20 Rejoice in labor, as a gift from God
Luke 12:30-31 World seeks after, but God knows needs
Psalm 37:28 Righteous inherit land and dwell there
1 Timothy 6:3 Soul not filled with good, no burial
Proverbs 13:22 Good inheritance children's children
Luke 9:60 Let dead bury their dead, follow me
Psalm 37:25 Not seen righteous forsaken, seed beg.

Is the typical retirement scriptural? Did anyone in the Bible retire? Was there a king, prophet or anyone else who retired? If only 71 percent of Americans reach retirement age, should we plan for it? If the church took care of widows and orphans, would we work when we are too ill or too weak? What about the claim that I could do so much more for God if I were retired?

Psalm 25:15 Plucked my feet out of the net.
Genesis 21:10 Cast out Hagar and Ishmael.
Ecclesiastes 6:3 Soul not filled with good, no burial.
Luke 9:60 Let dead bury their dead, follow me.
Luke 12:30-31 World seeks after, but God knows needs.
Psalm 37:28 Lord forsakes not saints.
Acts 8:20 Thought gift of God purchased money.

Why are children entitled to this money? Is it bad for society? Inheritance destroys drive and motivation to work. 55 percent federal tax 15 to 30 percent state tax. War in family. 29% die before age 65. 3% do not need help. Self worth not in your job. No taxes on gifts now. Trust arrangements, annuities which deny access to principal, can exclude Medicaid. Will, Durable power of attorney health care, Living Will, Single Premium Fixed Immediate Annuity. FDR 1930's social security created because of unemployment. Joint survivor charitable trust. Charitable remainder trust.

How To Prepare For Incapacity And Death, Including Retirement

Should a Christian prepare for the inevitable? What about the passage from this life to the next? How do I prepare for increasing age and retirement? Should I leave an inheritance to my children? Is there something more valuable than money that I could leave to them? Am I providing them with a temptation to incentives my demise? Was the old testament inheritance essentially a farm or ranch? Are we really talking about a way to survive?

Is a career or an education closer to that than dollars? If you earned the minimum wage, which is currently $5.15 per hour, that is only about $11,000 per year. Most earn more than that. The average household is currently earning $43,000. When the 2000 census is complete, we will have better figures to work with. At even $40,000, and working for 50 years that is $2,000,000. A millionaire two times over. As you can see, most Americans are millionaires. It just comes slowly.

If you start at age 25, and invest $2,000 per year in an IRA tax deferred mutual fund earning 12%, you will have $1.3 million at age 65. In other words, for about $150 per month, you can have $1.3 million. Of course, this assumes no withdrawals, no divorces, reinvested dividends and an average rate of return.

Consider the following:

Proverbs 19:14 House and riches are the inheritance of fathers and a prudent wife is from the Lord. From whom? Only the Lord can give you a good wife. You will not find her otherwise.

Ecclesiastes 5:14 A son can waste father's inheritance.

30 For all these things do the nations of the world seek after: and your Father knoweth that ye have need of these things.

31 But rather seek ye the kingdom of God; and all these things shall be added unto you.

Luke 12:30-31

28 For the LORD loveth judgment, and forsaketh not his saints; they are preserved for ever: but the seed of the wicked shall be cut off. Psalm 37:28 3 If a man beget an hundred children, and live many years, so that the days of his years be many, and his soul be not filled with good, and also that he have no burial; I say, that an untimely birth is better than he.

Ecclesiastes 6:3

8 But if any provide not for his own, and specially for those of his own house, he hath denied the faith, and is worse than an infidel.

1 Timothy 5:8

22 A good man leaveth an inheritance to his children's children: and the wealth of the sinner is laid up for the just.

Proverbs 13:22

60 Jesus said unto him, Let the dead bury their dead: but go thou and preach the kingdom of God.

Luke 9:60

25 I have been young, and now am old; yet have I not seen the righteous forsaken, nor his seed begging bread.

Psalm 37:25

IS RETIREMENT SCRIPTURAL?

Did anyone in the Bible retire? Was there a king, prophet or anyone else who retired?

If only 71 percent of Americans reach retirement age, should we plan for it?

If the church took care of widows and orphans, would we work when we are too ill or too weak? What about the claim that I could do so much more for God if I were retired?

Mine eyes are ever toward the LORD; for he shall pluck my feet out of the net. Psalm 25:15

Wherefore she said unto Abraham, Cast out this bondwoman and her son: for the son of this bondwoman shall not be heir with my son, even with Isaac. Genesis 21:10 If a man beget an hundred children, and live many years, so that the days of his years be many, and his soul be not filled with good, and also that he have no burial; I say, that an untimely birth is better than he. Ecclesiastes 6:3

Jesus said unto him, Let the dead bury their dead: but go thou and preach the kingdom of God. Luke 9:60

For all these things do the nations of the world seek after: and your Father knoweth that ye have need of these things.

31But rather seek ye the kingdom of God; and all these things shall be added unto you.

Luke 12:30-31

For the LORD loveth judgment, and forsaketh not his saints; they are preserved for ever: but the seed of the wicked shall be cut off. Psalm 37:28

But Peter said unto him, Thy money perish with thee, because thou hast thought that the gift of God may be purchased with money.

Acts 8:20

Why are children entitled to this money? Is it bad for

society? Does inheritance destroy drive and motivation to work?

Why do only 3% of Americans retire with enough money to survive?

There are no taxes on gifts now. Trust arrangements, annuities which deny access to principal, can be utilized to exclude Medicaid. How might this relate to me?

Will, Durable power of attorney health care, Living Will, Single Premium Fixed Immediate Annuities, could help me how?

What is a joint survivor charitable trust?

What is a charitable remainder trust?

How does Ecclesiastes 11 help me plan for retirement? Will God hold you accountable if you hide your head in the sand and say I am trusting the Lord?

Plan for the inevitable

CHAPTER 19

HOW TO ELIMINATE DEBT

Many people ask me how to invest. However, no counsel regarding the principles of investing, should be offered without first discussing how to save. And, no counsel regarding the principles of saving, should be offered without first discussing how to eliminate debt. Therefore, the final three chapters are on debt, saving and investing. And they must be accomplished in this order.

What is the difference between saving and investing. It is the difference between swimming and diving. With saving or swimming, it must become so comfortable and repetitious. It must be a habit. Only after swimming in water, should one attempt to dive in water. You must swim before you dive. You must save before you invest. Saving is living within your means. If you spend less than you earn you are by definition, saving. If you cannot live within your means you cannot save. If you cannot save, you cannot invest. If you are in debt you are not saving or investing. They are mutually exclusive. You are either in Heaven or Hell and cannot be in both places simultaneously.

Many have asked me where to invest or how to save. Yet they owe interest. Typically, your car financing is 18%, your credit card interest is 21%, and your home mortgage is 11%. Bank saving accounts pay 3%, and Certificate of Deposit (CD's) are currently paying 6%. Does it make sense to save or invest at 3 or 6%, and pay interest at the rate of 11, 18, or 21%? Therefore, the best investment you could make is to eliminate debt. Instead of earning 3%, you will begin to earn 21% overnight. How easy can this be. First, eliminate debt, then save, then invest.

10) When my son turned 16, I began to purchase department gift store gift cards for cash. He can buy school clothes, shoes etc. whatever he wants and must stay within the budget. Why because I do not shop with him. If he goes over budget, he must something back, as the clerk will not advance him any more than the card allows. This is also a good method for people who cannot be trusted with cash. Of course, they can return the item for cash, but if a teenager, the items will be worth more than cash. Of course, he has a savings account at the bank.

11) Never write an NSF check. Overdraft fees are very expensive. Some leave a balance of $100 in their account for this purpose. If you really have $600, merely write $500 in the check register.

12) Keep your checking account on computer. The $100 or so you spend on Quickbooks or something similar will save you far more than in NSF fees.

13) When you have to shop, shop with a friend who is cheaper than you. They will tell you no more often than you would.

14) Never shop when tired, hungry, sad, or angry. When a woman has a pity party she will spend $40 on a clothing item. When a man has one, he will buy a $4,000 motorcycle. Guys it is cheaper to just make her happy. And ladies, it is far cheaper if you keep the husband happy. Most of my debt counseling uncovers the man at fault.

15) Learn to sew and iron your clothes.

16) Learn to polish shoes.

17) Learn to rent movies at 99 cents instead of spending $15 for a night at the movie theater.

18) Learn to eat at home. We eat out for special occasions such as Mother's day or birthdays. However, if you eat out every day, you have wasted $1,500 per adult per year. If your family eats out every week you have wasted $2000.

19) Find the library and read books for free. But what about Christian books? Does your church have a library? If you need a Christian book, it would only be a book on a subject your pastor never preaches on (like this book). Otherwise, get his tapes for free.

20) Take no vacations or trips unless they are at least in part tax deductible.

21) And finally, try the 72 hour rule. Every time you want or need something, wait 72 hours before you buy it. This technique alone will save you over $2,000 per year.

Consider the following:

Luke 8:18 Whoever has shall be given and who has not it shall be taken from him. Now that you have read this far, you are accountable for what you have read.

Luke 12:18 Are you laying up earthly treasure? The Lord called him a fool His society called him successful.

Luke 19:26 Whoever has shall be given and who has not it shall be taken from him.

Luke 22:36 Planning is essential.

1 Corinthians 3:13 Every person's life will be made known.

2 Corinthians 9:11 As you give, God will get the glory.

1 Timothy 6:18 Be rich in good works.

James 1:2-3 Count it all joy when you have trials.

What percent of current income is necessary to save in order to send one child to college? The budgeting example in the back of this book suggests 10%. Of course that is a debt free budget, so that must be accomplished first. And it also assumes reinvestment in the career before paying for college. Prepaid college tuition plans are available in every state. This is much cheaper than saving and paying the rates in effect at that time. I paid 100% of my college, graduate school and post-graduate expenses. They were not expensive schools but the University of Texas, George Mason University, and the University of North Texas are all members of the American Assemblies of College Schools of Business (AACSB). In other words, the elite.

However, is a college education a parental responsibility? That is not a Christian right of children. This is an American tradition. Save for the sake of saving. God will show you how to spend it. The spending is the easy part.

What does it mean to ignore the new and repair before replace? Be content in whatever state you are in. Be a good steward of what the Lord has given you. Instead of neglecting and abusing your old lawnmower, maintain it. That is cheaper than buying a new one. If you must buy one, buy the durable type even if it costs more initially. If it lasts longer before replacement, you have saved more than the initial difference in cost.

Proverbs 22:3 Wise man foresees the evil and hides himself but simple pass on, punished. How do I eliminate debt. Debt is a spiritual condition. If you have a debt, it is because you rejected the provision God made for you. You were not happy with what God provided and you did not need his help to get what you wanted. Why? Each time God said no, Visa, Mastercard, and Discover came along and said you can have it now painlessly. The bible says there is pleasure in sin for a season. When God says no to you, you overrule Him in your life. How did he say no? Did He provide the resources to buy that item? If not, then He told you no. But you don't like that.

What is the difference between lusting for a material possession and lusting for someone else's wife? Either way God told you no. But you want what you want when you want it. You may not care what God says. Then when you are deep in debt, you ask the church and the pastor to pray to God to rescue you. How can he rescue you? You are his child. He must teach you a lesson so this never happens again. If it took years to get into debt it will take years to get out. If it took months to get in it will take months to get out.

The only Christian who is truly trusting God with their material resources is the Christian who is debt free. In addition, being in debt disqualifies you from spiritual leadership. A pastor, elder, and deacon, must be blameless and above reproach. Read the requirements in Ephesians for church leadership. How can someone in debt qualify? The mere fact that they are in debt either means they cannot control their own earthly desires, or they are not the head of their own household. This should be a question in every ordination, or selection interview.

A few related verses follow.

Genesis 45:18 living well.

Who can live better than a believer? At any level of income.

Proverbs 16:3 Commit works unto the Lord.

Proverbs 16:9 The Lord directs his steps.

Can anyone expect to make it without the Lord's help?

Proverbs 21:20 Wise man saves.

Proverbs 24:3-4 Wisdom is a house built.

Proverbs 27:24 Riches are not forever.

For the past 16 years, I have been teaching the principles in this book in churches, and Christian conferences. Many have asked for practical suggestions on how to eliminate debt. Try some of these ideas:

1) Cut your credit cards up and throw them away. Write a letter to each company canceling the cards. Please remember that criminals are watching for credit card numbers that used to have activity. They are prime targets for fraudulent thefts. If you want to quit smoking drinking or using drugs would you leave those products in the house? No, of course not. Debt is a sin, which is just as difficult to overcome.

2) Cut up your automatic teller and automatic money machine cards. These cash withdrawals provide no audit trail and therefore no accountability. You will not win over debt unless you know where your money is being spent.

3) Determine how much you owe and to whom. You may be surprised. Include the Internal Revenue Service because they come first.

4) If married, discuss the list with your spouse. Then get on your knees and confess this sin, and ask forgiveness

from God. Forgiveness because you did not trust him before.

5)   Pay every creditor at least five dollars per month. This will look better on your credit report. Equifax, Experian and Trans Union are the three credit services. It costs $8 each to write for a report. Or you can obtain a combined one on the Internet for $29.95. You can use the American Express card since they require payment in full each month. If you have enough to pay more than $5, pay the smallest debts first. This will encourage you to continue. Remember, debt elimination is financial dieting. The first two weeks on any debt are the most agonizing.

6)   Open your mail every day standing next to a trash can. Unsolicited credit card offers are received daily at our house. I shred them in the trash without opening them.

7)   Stop subscribing or reading magazines. Every other page is something you neither needed or wanted before reading it. Even Christian magazines contain so much advertising that you will be tempted. Television is something to be concerned about as well. I watch football on television. The commercials are either for alcoholic beverages or for automobiles. Since I have never had a drop to drink, and I am 44, this is easy to ignore. However, sometimes that Lexus or Mercedes looks good to me. Yet, In my spirit I know I would not buy one even if I had the cash.

8)   Never go to a shopping mall without a written list, and a budget. And never walk in any store other than the one the list previously agreed to. The mall is designed to persuade you or trick you into parting with your money. Be realistic. If you needed it you would not need the store to tell you that you needed it. No advertising would be necessary. The fact that they are advertising to you means you do not need it. The same rules apply for grocery store or drug store shopping.

9) Never take a child or teenager to a shopping mall. If you as an adult Christian cannot guard yourself against the wiles of the devil, why do you expect your child to so do so? No wonder children cry at the store. It is painful for them. You took them to a wonderful place that can satisfy all of their human desires and now you will not complete the transaction by buying it for them. And, this is not the place to teach them about money. You teach a young person about money by their spending time with poor people. Poor people manage money better than the rich.

CHAPTER 20

HOW TO SAVE

Now that you are on the way to eliminating debt, we can continue saving. Continue? You are already saving if you are minimizing debt. You see managing money is pure algebra. If you stop one thing you have started another. If not negative, then positive. The moment you minimized debt is the moment you began to save. Congratulations, you are on your way to a happier and better life.

Comment on the following:

Isaiah 55:2 Wherefore do you spend money for that which is not bread? and your labor for that which satisfies not?

Mark 4:19 Cares of this world.

Luke 3:11 Wants deemed as a surplus of goods.

Luke 21:34 Be on guard against the cares of this life.

Philippians 4:11 Contentment.

1 Peter 3:7 Husbands are to love their wives.

Steps toward a savings lifestyle:

1)   Pay cash for everything, or as much as possible.
2)   Every evening, when returning home, place the coins in a piggy bank, receptacle, or one of those that divides and rolls the coins.
3)   At the end of each month you will have approximately $30 to $50.
4)   Once a month, take the coins to the bank. They

can roll them. Deposit that amount into the savings account, not the checking account.

5) $100 will be necessary to open the account, so the first few months you may not be able to go to the bank.

6)   Congratulate yourself when the account is opened. In the 1970 census, 97% of the nations household had television sets. 96% had indoor plumbing. You are now in the small group that has a savings account. I prefer banks to credit unions because credit is more difficult to obtain in a bank.

7)   Try an automatic monthly transfer from checking to savings. If necessary, start with the bank minimum.

8)   If steps one through seven had been successful for 6 months, increase the monthly transfer by at least $50. Continue this process until you have over $5,000 in the account.

9)   After reaching $5,000, move to a certificate of deposit. But what if I need the money? Use it. That is why we are saving. This is the way God provides for his people. If you do not need it, move it to the CD. Select the CD with the best rate. This will mean the longest term and the greatest penalty for early withdrawal. This is precisely what we want Make it inconvenient to withdraw. I like for people to choose a bank that closes early and does not have a drive through window. This makes it less likely you will withdraw your money.

10) Each time, $5,000 is accumulated, purchase another CD.

When do I invest the money? First, become debt free. Second, save. Third, invest. If you have $20,000 in the bank that you have no immediate need for, plan the next several years. If you have a need for that money, plan the CD's so that they mature in time for that need. If you have done all this and do not need the money for a few years, you are ready to invest.

Saving for Major Needs
BUDGETING

Proverbs 16:3 Commit works unto the Lord.

Proverbs 16:9 The Lord directs his steps.

Proverbs 24:3-4 Wisdom is a house built.

James 1:2-3 My brethren, count it all joy when ye fall into divers temptations;

3Knowing this, that the trying of your faith worketh patience.

Proverbs 16:3 Commit works to Lord.

Proverbs 16:9 Man's heart devises.

Proverbs 3:9-10 Honour the LORD with thy substance, and with the firstfruits of all thine increase:

10So shall thy barns be filled with plenty, and thy presses shall burst out with new wine.

2 Corinthians 9:11 Being enriched in every thing to all bountifulness, which causeth through us thanksgiving to God.

Proverbs 21:20 There is treasure to be desired and oil in the dwelling of the wise; but a foolish man spendeth it up.

Proverbs 27:23 24 Be thou diligent to know the state of thy flocks, and look well to thy herds.

24For riches are not for ever: and doth the crown endure to every generation?

18 That they do good, that they be rich in good works, ready to distribute, willing to communicate;

19 Laying up in store for themselves a good foundation against the time to come, that they may lay hold on eternal life.

1 Timothy 6:18-19

Luke 8:18 18Take heed therefore how ye hear: for whosoever hath, to him shall be given; and whosoever hath not, from him shall be taken even that which he seemeth to have.

Luke 19:26 Luke 19:26

26 For I say unto you, That unto every one which hath shall be given; and from him that hath not, even that he hath shall be taken away from him.

1 Corinthians 3:131

13Every man's work shall be made manifest: for the day shall declare it, because it shall be revealed by fire; and the fire shall try every man's work of what sort it is.

Proverbs 13:22 A good man leaveth an inheritance to his children's children: and the wealth of the sinner is laid up for the just.

Proverbs 21:20 Wise man saves.

Genesis 45:18 Living well.

Luke 22:36 Planning.

Luke 12:18 And he said, This will I do: I will pull down my barns, and build greater; and there will I bestow all my fruits and my goods.

Proverbs 22:3 A prudent man foreseeth the evil, and hideth himself: but the simple pass on, and are punished.

Getting ready for the Tax Return Preparation.

Whether you prepare your own returns, use a software program or hire someone else, the following list will help you get ready:

Social security numbers for every member of the family.

Childcare costs and providers' names, addresses and tax ID or social security numbers.

Education costs for anything past high school for any member of the family.

Adoption costs and related expenses including transportation.

Income including all W-2s or 1099's.

Investment income on 1099's, K-1's or even on a W-2 for some employee stock transactions.

Income tax refunds.

Alimony paid.

Business or farm income.

If a home is used for business, an allocation of square footage and all home expenses.

IRA and pension distributions including 1099's and an 8606 if appropriate.

Rental property income and expenses.

Unemployment income.

Social security benefits.

Income from sales of property.

Miscellaneous income such as jury duty and gambling winnings and prizes, etc.

Saving for Minor Wants

Isaiah 55:2 Wherefore do you spend money for that which is not bread? and your labor for that which satisfies not?

Hearken diligently unto me and eat you that which is good, and let your soul delight in fatness.

Mark 4:19 Cares of this world.

Philippians 4:11 Contentment.

1 Peter 3:7 Husbands are to love their wives.

Luke 3:11 Wants defined as a surplus of goods

Saving for Major Wants

Luke 6:24-25 But woe unto you that are rich! for ye have received your consolation.

25 Woe unto you that are full! for ye shall hunger. Woe unto you that laugh now! for ye shall mourn and weep.

1 Corinthians 3:12-13 Now if any man build upon this foundation gold, silver, precious stones, wood, hay, stubble;

13 Every man's work shall be made manifest: for the day shall declare it, because it shall be revealed by fire; and the fire shall try every man's work of what sort it is.

Luke 12:15 And he said unto them, Take heed, and beware of covetousness: for a man's life consisteth not in the abundance of the things which he possesseth.

For the sun is no sooner risen with a burning heat, but it withereth the grass, and the flower thereof falleth, and the grace of the fashion of it perisheth: so also shall the rich man fade away in his ways.1 Timothy 6:10

Ecclesiastes 5:13 13There is a sore evil which I have seen under the sun, namely, riches kept for the owners thereof to their hurt.

1 John 2:15-1615Love not the world, neither the things that are in the world. If any man love the world, the love of the Father is not in him.

16 For all that is in the world, the lust of the flesh, and the lust of the eyes, and the pride of life, is not of the Father, but is of the world.

ENVY

Proverbs 3:10. So shall thy barns be filled with plenty, and thy presses shall burst out with new wine.

Psalm 49:16-17 Be not thou afraid when one is made rich, when the glory of his house is increased;

17 For when he dieth he shall carry nothing away: his glory shall not descend after him.

Hebrews 13:5 Let your conversation be without covetousness; and be content with such things as ye have: for he hath said, I will never leave thee, nor forsake thee.

Riches and honour are with me; yea, durable riches and righteousness.

19 My fruit is better than gold, yea, than fine gold; and my revenue than choice silver.

20 I lead in the way of righteousness, in the midst of the paths of judgment:

21That I may cause those that love me to inherit substance; and I will fill their treasures.

Proverbs 8:18-21

The hand of the diligent shall bear rule: but the slothful shall be under tribute. Proverbs 12:24

When pride cometh, then cometh shame: but with the lowly is wisdom. Proverbs 11:2

Wealth gotten by vanity shall be diminished: but he that gathereth by labour shall increase. Proverbs 13:11

Covetousness

1 Peter 3:3-4 Lifestyle of moderation.

Ephesians 5:5 Covetous man no part in the kingdom.

James 4:3 Ask that may consume it on your lusts.

Job 21:17 Calamity will come upon the greedy.

And he said unto them, Take heed, and beware of covetousness: for a man's life consisteth not in the abundance of the things which he possesseth. Luke 12:15

2 But as for me, my feet were almost gone; my steps had well nigh slipped. 3For I was envious at the foolish, when I saw the prosperity of the wicked. Psalm 73:2-3

But now I have written unto you not to keep company, if any man that is called a brother be a fornicator, or covetous, or an idolator, or a railer, or a drunkard, or an extortioner; with such an one no not to eat. 1 Corinthians 5:11

3 Let nothing be done through strife or vainglory; but in lowliness of mind let each esteem other better than themselves. Philippians 2:3

5 But ye say, Whosoever shall say to his father or his mother, It is a gift, by whatsoever thou mightest be profited by me;

6 And honour not his father or his mother, he shall be free. Thus have ye made the commandment of God of none effect by your tradition. Matthew 15:5-6 1

8 But if any provide not for his own, and especially for those of his own house, he hath denied the faith, and is worse than an infidel. Timothy 5:8

Luke 8:14 And that which fell among thorns are they, which, when they have heard, go forth, and are choked with cares and riches and pleasures of this life, and bring no fruit to perfection.

Overindulgence

Luke 12:15 Warned to beware of greed.

But godliness with contentment is great gain. 1 Timothy 6:6

Proverbs 23:17 Let not thine heart envy sinners: but be thou in the fear of the LORD all the day long.

Proverbs 17:12 Fool in his folly. Luke 16:10-12

Psalm 73:2-3 Slipping from God's path. Matthew 20:15-16

For the sun is no sooner raised with a burning heat, but it withereth the grass, and the flower thereof falleth, and the grace of the fashion of it perisheth: so also shall the rich man fade away in his ways. James 1:11

26 For God giveth to a man that is good in his sight wisdom, and knowledge, and joy: but to the sinner he giveth travail, to gather and to heap up that he may give to him that is good before God. This also is vanity and vexation of spirit.

22 The blessing of the LORD, it maketh rich, and he addeth no sorrow with it.

Proverbs 10:22

16 Be of the same mind one toward another. Mind not high things, but condescend to men of low estate. Be not wise in your own conceits.

Romans 12:16

3 Let nothing be done through strife or vainglory; but in lowliness of mind let each esteem other better than themselves.

4 Look not every man on his own things, but every man also on the things of others.

5 Let this mind be in you, which was also in Christ Jesus:

Philippians 2:3-5

1 From whence come wars and fightings among you? come they not hence, even of your lusts that war in your members?

2 Ye lust, and have not: ye kill, and desire to have, and cannot obtain: ye fight and war, yet ye have not, because ye ask not.

James 4:1-2

19 For though I be free from all men, yet have I made myself servant unto all, that I might gain the more.

1 Corinthians 9:19

If we borrow money, where is the trust in God to provide for our needs? Why would we ask God to provide for our needs, if Visa and Mastercard can do it without being asked?

Old Testament on Wealth

Deuteronomy 8:18 That gives you power to get wealth.
2 Kings 4:1-7 Elisha and miraculous provisions.
1 Chronicles 29:12 Riches come from God.
Job 31:24-25 Placing confidence in wealth.
Psalm 4:1 1Hear me when I call, O God of my righteousness: thou hast enlarged me when I was in distress; have mercy upon me, and hear my prayer.
Psalm 19:10 Desiring wealth.

MAJOR WANTS

Can we have these things? Are they sins? Is there an opportunity cost? What choices are we making? What are the consequences of those decisions later?
23But he turned, and said unto Peter, Get thee behind me, Satan: thou art an offence unto me: for thou savourest not the things that be of God, but those that be of men.

CHAPTER 21

HOW TO INVEST

How do I accomplish the transition from saving to investing? Remember the example of the contrast between swimming and diving. It is a risk reward paradigm. The risk of diving is greater than that of swimming. However, the reward (at least to young people) is also much greater. Saving has very little risk and a small reward (maybe only 6%).

Your money will grow faster if is invested in mutual funds or corporate stocks or bonds. With an automatic monthly debt transfer from your checking account, some funds will let you in for $25 or $50 per month, many ask then about the timing of the purchases. What if my transfer is on the day when the price is high? Ignore that. Dollar cost averaging is what they taught us in business school. It means that a regular and systematic investment strategy is wiser than timing the market for those purchases. Of course, it was based upon the Bible verse, steady plodding brings prosperity. I did not offer that to my Finance professors, nor did I mention it in secular universities. When I taught at Christian universities, this connection could be articulated.

The next question is what we invest in. As there are hundreds of thousands of stocks, thousands of mutual funds and numerous bonds, which one is right for you. Remember your DNA, voiceprint, and fingerprints? You are unique. So is everyone else. You cannot invest based upon what someone else does. If you try to follow someone else you will never achieve the results they achieve. It must be unique to you. Every investment strategy must be unique to the individual.

How do l decide which one to invest in? Simple. What is your set of knowledge, skills, abilities, gifts, talents and" education? What do you know more than "others?" My expertise is in medical group practice management. Therefore, I chose a mutual fund that invests in health science corporate stocks. I also have taught computer systems analysis so I have another investment in a mutual fund that invests in emerging technologies. These types of investments are not right for you. My grandfather—purchased General Motors stock because he was a traveling auto parts salesman, and also the wisest person I ever met. A man who with a ninth grade education gave his two sons a start in their careers. My grandmother worked for J. C. Penny's and invested through the employee stock option plan. I am a strong proponent of people purchasing stock in the company they work for. First, you know what makes the stock price go up or down and when. Second, anytime a company matches investments even in part, your rate of return just skyrocketed.

Investing therefore requires a self-appraisal. God gave you something other people do not have. You have an advantage in investing if you stay with your own talents. What if you have done this and cannot come up with anything. Try harder. Do you really think God would have created you and not given you some talent? Use it not only in your career and helping people but also in investing. Most people disconnect their investments from the people God made them to be. Why?

Once the investment is made, leave it alone. Do not call your broker. Do not read the stock quotes on TV or in the newspaper. And do not read magazines for investment advice, by the time you read it is too late. The smart people have made their move before the magazine was mailed. And you are too easily influenced by it. Finally, what makes you think they know what they are talking about? When I worked for the Civil Aeronautics board (now the Department of Transportation), magazine journalists visited my office almost weekly when writing their stories. Most of the time the young people knew almost nothing about the airline business. Yet, their article would influence millions of people to buy or sell airline stocks. If you are a Christian, you must search for truth. And you must be able to recognize it. What you read other than the Bible, it is just some persons opinion of the truth.

Based upon Ecclesiastes 11:1-2, answer the following questions:

1) Why do we invest? Because we know we will need to spend that money someday for a legitimate purpose.

2) What do we invest in? Our best guesses of what we know. If we know when it will go up or down and when.

3) When do we invest? Regularly. As a part of a disciplined lifestyle.

4) How do we invest? Eight different pots. Business, House, IRA, CD's, mutual funds, savings account, etc.

5) How do we train our children to invest? By example. Not by telling them no. By showing them how to say no to yourself and still be happy.

There are some other verses which help us learn to invest. 20 A faithful man shall abound with blessings: but he that maketh haste to be rich shall not be innocent.

21 To have respect of persons is not good: for a piece of bread that man will transgress.

22 He that hasteth to be rich hath an evil eye, and considereth not that poverty shall come upon him. Proverbs 28:20. In the secular world, this is described as dollar cost averaging. Or explained more fully, it is the practice of making routine and small economic decisions which over time pay off well. In other words more right decisions than wrong. The alternative philosophy is trying to hit a home run instead of a base hit, every time at bat.

19 Lay not up for yourselves treasures upon earth, where

moth and rust doth corrupt, and where thieves break through and steal:

20 But lay up for yourselves treasures in heaven, where neither moth nor rust doth corrupt, and where thieves do not break through nor steal:

21 For where your treasure is, there will your heart be also.

22 The light of the body is the eye: if therefore thine eye be single, thy whole body shall be full of light.

23 But if thine eye be evil, thy whole body shall be full of darkness. If therefore the light that is in thee be darkness, how great is that darkness!

24 No man can serve two masters: for either he will hate the one, and love the other; or else he will hold to the one, and despise the other. Ye cannot serve God and mammon.

25 Therefore I say unto you, Take no thought for your life, what ye shall eat, or what ye shall drink; nor yet for your body, what ye shall put on. Is not the life more than meat, and the body than raiment?

26 Behold the fowls of the air: for they sow not, neither do they reap, nor gather into barns; yet your heavenly Father feedeth them. Are ye not much better than they?

27 Which of you by taking thought can add one cubit unto his stature?

28 And why take ye thought for raiment? Consider the lilies of the field, how they grow; they toil not, neither do they spin:

29 And yet I say unto you, That even Solomon in all his glory was not arrayed like one of these.

30 Wherefore, if God so clothe the grass of the field, which to day is, and to morrow is cast into the oven, shall he not much more clothe you, O ye of little faith?

31 Therefore take no thought, saying, What shall we eat? or, What shall we drink? or, Wherewithal shall we be clothed?

32 (For after all these things do the Gentiles seek:) for your heavenly Father knoweth that ye have need of all these things.

33 But seek ye first the kingdom of God, and his righteousness; and all these things shall be added unto you.

34 Take therefore no thought for the morrow: for the

morrow shall take thought for the things of itself. Sufficient unto the day is the evil thereof.

Matthew 6:19-34

24 But woe unto you that are rich! for ye have received your consolation.

25 Woe unto you that are full! for ye shall hunger. Woe unto you that laugh now! for ye shall mourn and weep.

Luke 6:24-25

A faithful man shall abound with blessings, but he that makes haste to be rich shall not be innocent. Respect of persons is not good, for a piece of bread...He that hastens to be rich, has an evil eye, and considers not that poverty shall come upon him. Set your affection on things above. Woe unto you that are rich. (Never been a rich soul winner). Poor of this world are rich in faith. Which would you rather be? A man's life does not consist in the abundance of things that he possesses.

One of my best friends in high school, responded when I quoted this verse. He said his life does consist of the things he possesses. And he said this after his van his prized possession was totaled and he was in recovery from his injuries,

Read the following verses in light of the envy in your own heart. To what extent are you envious?

Psalm 49:16-17 Be not afraid when one is made rich for when he dies he shall carry nothing away.

Pastor Neal Jones was fond of saying he never saw a hearse pulling a u-haul trailer. Alexander the great ruler who at age 33, owned or ruled two thirds of the world's land mass, ordered his generals to bury him palms turned up. Then they were to make his millions of soldiers walk by look at his palms and ponder what he took with him. J. P. Morgan, the wealthy industrialist of early US history, gave none of his estate to relatives. He did not want to deprive them of the joy of earning one themselves.

Proverbs 11:2 When pride comes then comes shame Proverbs 12:24 Hand of diligent bear rule Proverbs 13:11 Wealth gotten by vanity shall be diminished but he that gathers by labor shall increase.

Hebrews 13:5 Let your conversation be without

covetousness, and be content with such things as you have, for he has said, I will never leave you, nor forsake you.

Investing for future needs is the ultimate step on the stairway to financial maturity. It can only be accomplished with discipline over many years.

Read the following verses in light of covetousness:

Job 21:17 Calamity will come upon the greedy.

Psalm 73:2 Envious at the foolish.

One year I was honored to substitute for our pastor. On one of those occasions, I preached on Psalm 73. I did not know if I affected anyone, but I was delayed leaving when so many wanted to respond personally. If you are concerned with what everyone else has, you are never going to be happy with what God gives you.

24 If I have made gold my hope, or have said to the fine gold, Thou art my confidence;

25 If I rejoice because my wealth was great, and because mine hand had gotten much;

Job 31:24-25

1 Hear me when I call, O God of my righteousness: thou hast enlarged me when I was in distress; have mercy upon me, and hear my prayer.

Psalm 4:1

10 More to be desired are they than gold, yea, than much fine gold: sweeter also than honey and the honeycomb.

Psalm 19:10

6 Pray for the peace of Jerusalem: they shall prosper that love thee.

7 Peace be within thy walls, and prosperity within thy palaces.

Psalm 122:6-7

The following four verses are merely cautionary. They remind us of what we already know about ourselves. Perhaps, they will cause us to slow down in overspending. Dr. Visser, a great Dutch evangelist, used to say, "Starve the Old Nature,

Feed the New". His life was chronicled in the book, Behind the Iron Curtain, written by A. H. Barbee.

Proverbs 17:12 Fool in his folly.

Luke 8:14 Overindulgence.

Ephesians 5:5 Covetous man no part in the kingdom.

James 4:3 Ask that may consume it on your lusts.

1 Peter 3:3-4 Lifestyle of moderation.

If we borrow money, where is the trust in God to provide for our needs? Why would we ask God to provide for our needs, if Visa and Mastercard can do it without our Lord being asked?

Deuteronomy 8:18 That gives you power to get wealth.

2 Kings 4:1-7 Elisha and miraculous provisions.

1 Chronicles 29:12 Riches come from God.

One possible conclusion from reading these three verses is that we should have a certain peace about our financial situation. We may never be a number one draft choice and receive $25 million. However, God has given us as much as He wants us to manage.

What people see may not be the truth. Those that look successful may not be and vise versa.

CHAPTER 22

CONCLUSION

The authors have attempted in one volume to address every financial decision in life and share what the Bible has to say. Some would describe this as impossible. Others might say it is Herculean. We think we can help the reader get started with the philosophy that the Bible has the answers. At the end of this book, we have included a few frequently asked questions.

Also, we want to provide you with a concise step by step cheat sheet and this follows.

In chapter one, we suggested that you start talking about money and confronting those personal issues. We thought you should involve your spouse or parents or someone you trust, in this exercise.

In Chapter 2, we linked money and spirituality. We established that there is a link because the checkbook will always reflect what is in a person's heart.

In Chapter 3, we established priorities for giving to the work of the Lord as well as who not to give to. With so many deserving and undeserving choices, we provided guidance as to how to make those decisions.

In Chapter 4, we expanded upon how Christians should operate in the financial realm. A financial decision can in fact be a spiritual decision and oftentimes is.

In Chapter 5, we encouraged readers to be responsible with money and even to build wealth slowly in a deliberate and disciplined fashion.

In Chapter 6, we looked at a Biblical view of prosperity. We said there is no sin in earning a profit and building wealth.

In Chapter 7, we gave a Budgeting example and discussed insurance and credit.

In Chapter 8, we advised readers how to choose their counselors. We said the choice of a counselor may be one of the most important financial decisions ever made.

In Chapter 9, we explained why the first check or payment always goes to God. It is an act of worship and is more than symbolic. It establishes our priorities and the proper order for using our wealth.

In Chapter 10, we described the mechanics of spiritual giving.

In Chapter 11, we gave examples of Christian giving.

In Chapter 12, we helped the reader gain an understanding of spending priorities.

In Chapter 13, we gave Biblical references that suggest food and clothing are the second and third priorities.

In Chapter 14, we talked about earning money. We said that earning money was more important than spending money. And we explained that there is an investment required in oneself and that this is the fourth priority.

In Chapter 15, we looked at Transportation issues and connected them to the earning money issues in the previous chapter.

In Chapter 16, we emphasized insurance and medical care as priorities and necessities. We also offered some solutions as to how to save money in these areas.

In Chapter 17, we described the need for a house and how best to pay for one. We saw houses as necessities and not investments. We placed housing as the seventh most important priority.

In Chapter 18, we spoke of the inevitable demise of each of us and how best to prepare for those tasks.

In Chapter 19, we described debt as something to be very cautiously used. And we suggested ways to minimize or reduce or eliminate debt.

In Chapter 20, we stated that a Christian can have some of the things they want in life. And that God is not trying to keep us from having a good life.

In Chapter 21, we spoke of investing and explained the Biblical patterns of investing. One of those is dollar cost averaging or a disciplined approach. Another is having all of our money in eight different buckets.

In Chapter 22, we summarized. We do not expect that everyone will master every technique the first time the book is read. However, we do believe this can be a valuable reference guide to any reader. And we trust that the Lord will bless that portion of this book that contains His Word.

Frequently Asked Questions

1. My husband and I are interested in creating a simple budget but do not know where to begin. He does not have a steady income but works as needed. When he works he is well paid but it is hard to know when the money will come. I also work part-time but receive the same amount each week. When we do get paid, we tend to pay the biggest bills but always seem to be behind. Signed—Bewildered by Budgeting

Dear Bewildered,

Your family situation is not that unusual. I have seen many in the same circumstances. Start with looking at your total gross income on last year's income tax return (Form 1040). Divide that number by twelve to get a monthly income estimate. This is the amount you budget for in terms of income. Every dollar earned over that average can be used to diminish your debts.

Now let's discuss the expense side of the budget. You do not know how much you spend because it is spent in spurts, after each big payday for your husband. However, you do know how much you spend because you probably spend more than you earn. Budget your expenses for the same amount as the income.

For example, let's say that the household income is $7,000 per month. That amount must also be the total budgeted expenses for the month.

The next step is to divide the $7,000 of expenses into categories (taxes, debt reduction, savings, mortgage or rent automotive, groceries, etc.) At this point, you probably do not know how much to put in each category. Just to get started, you can estimate them by amount or percentage. These can be refined later. Most people do not start budgeting because they cannot be precise. The key is to start somewhere and continuously improve. By monitoring your progress each month together, you will be on your way to better manage all financial decisions.

Question 2

I read that the child tax credit is going to be $1,000 per child per year for several years. Is that true? Does that mean that my tax liability is reduced by that amount?

For calendar years 2005 through 2010, there will be a child tax credit of $1,000 per child per year. I make no predictions for the years beyond 2010. And yes it does mean that your tax due is reduced by that amount. That is the difference between a credit and a deduction. A credit is worth more since it is a dollar for dollar offset of taxes due and payable. A deduction on the other hand merely reduces the amount of money that the taxes are based upon.

For example, interest expense is of no taxable benefit if one utilizes the standard deduction, which most people do. If one itemizes deductions on Schedule A, then one merely reduces taxable income. Consider the case where a family has $12,000 in allowable interest on Schedule A and adjusted gross income of $80,000. This would mean that the taxes are calculated on $68,000 rather than $80,000. If a person were in a ten percent tax bracket, the $12,000 in interest only saved them $1,200 in taxes ($12,000 times ten percent).

The bottom line here is that the tax consequences can never be used to justify indebtedness.

Question 3

I never know if my boyfriend and I should file as single, or married filing jointly or married filing separately or head of household. We could get married if it would help save on our taxes. Which way gets us the biggest refund?

If you are not married yet, I would not suggest that income taxes affect your decision. The tax consequences of the marital status are usually less than one percent of the total lost by each party in a divorce. Therefore, let us not confuse marriage with income tax strategy.

If you get married, it is usually better to file a joint return. One instance where a separate filing is advised is when one party has a high income and also high deductions. Also, if a married couple is already physically separated and contemplating divorce, a married filing separately status is well advised.

If one parent has children from a previous marriage, and they qualify as dependent children, it is often preferable for that parent to file as head of household.

The bottom line is that some credits and benefits are only available to couples filing jointly. One way to determine is to ask your tax preparer or software program to produce "what if" tax returns. Whichever way yields the biggest refund is probably the winner.

Question 4

My wife and I are considering investing in an IRA. We are not sure if this will help our income tax situation and also do not know how to start. Can you please advise us about IRA's?

To get the maximum tax benefit, you and your wife can contribute up to $3,000 each per year but there are several limitations. If one or both of you is 50 or over, you can make a catch-up contribution of $500.

Whether or not you can deduct a traditional IRA contribution, depends upon your income and your employer retirement plan.

Roth IRA contributions are not deductible but they are my favorite. I prefer Roth IRA's because they accumulate tax deferred and can oftentimes be withdrawn tax-free.

Before we can discuss tax strategy surrounding retirement plans, we have to discuss investment strategy in general. And before we can discuss investments, we have to discuss debt. First, one must reduce the debt before investing. It makes no sense to earn one percent in interest while paying 21 percent in credit card interest. So pay off the debts first. When you are debt free or closer to it, start saving. Save any amount of money with any frequency just to get started.

There are some starter mutual funds, which will allow $25 or $50 per month to begin an account. These can oftentimes be styled as an IRA. The amount is not so important. The way to build wealth is start early and save often.

A 12% annual return on a mutual fund with $2,000 invested per year for forty years would yield over $1.3 million. If you can save $167 per month, earn 12%, and leave it alone for forty years, you will be a millionaire.

Dear Richard,

I get so confused about the tax calendar. I filed an automatic extension request and know it is due on or before August 15th. I owe money with that return for last year. Also, I seem to recall something about an estimated tax payment due September 15. Are those related? If I pay the first, do I need to pay the second?

Harmon

Dear Harmon,

The two dates have no relationship. The August 15th date relates to the previous calendar year. The September 15th date relates to the current calendar year. Based upon the comments you made, you will need to send in a check each of those consecutive months.

Richard

Money Question 6
Dear Richard,

I am purchasing a house and evaluating a comparison between 15 and 30 year mortgages. The principal of $150,000.00 is paid in both examples.

Al

Dear Al,

By paying the mortgage off in 15 years, the principal is paid in 15 rather than 30. $59,909.40 would have to be paid over the 15 year period in the form of higher monthly payments. The bottom line is choosing the 15 year option saves $138,206.80. At 8%, the savings almost equal the cost of the house!

Of course, a mortgage of any term can be paid down early by paying more than required. The essential difference is one of risk. With a shorter term, the lending institution can measure their risk/reward decision model better.

Richard

Money Question 7
Dear Richard,

I am confused about the IRA rules. I have tried to research the issue on the Internet but cannot tell if I have contributed too much. And if I did contribute too much, how do I correct it?

Dear Jimmie,

Here are a few thoughts to help you through the IRA rules and regulations:

If a taxpayer inadvertently contributes above the maximum, nondeductible contributions could be claimed for the traditional IRA or correcting the Roth IRA contribution could be done before April 15th. A taxpayer can contribute to both a traditional IRA and a Roth IRA in the same tax year. However, the annual dollar maximum was $2,000.00 for 2001, and $3,000.00 for 2002 and succeeding years, and $3,500 if over age 50. For calendar year 2005, this went to $4,000.00 per spouse and $4,500 if a person is over 50. That means a maximum for those married filing jointly of $8,000.00, $8,500.00 or $9,000.00. Withdrawals for both IRA types can begin at 59 and ½. Contributions to a traditional IRA can continue until 70 and ½. There is no age limit on Roth IRA contributions. Withdrawals must be made from traditional IRA's beginning at 70 and ½. Withdrawals have no time or amount restrictions on Roth IRA's. Traditional IRA withdrawals before 59 and ½ have 10% penalties, except for that invested only two years or less and that is 25%. and, If you don't take the minimum amount out of a traditional IRA, there is a 50% penalty on the difference between what should have been taken out and what was taken.

Richard

8. I'm 18 years old but am still in high school. I have no job and live with my parents. Can I open my own checking account?

A.   Visit your local bank. This will be more effective than calling. You do not have to know much about it. They will guide you. You might consider a parent with signature authority. That way they can assist with banking needs if you are away at college. I would reject the ATM card as premature. Learn how to manage the account first without the ATM card.

9. I think all banks are the same so perhaps I am going to pick the most convenient location?

A.   The most important question is whether or not there is a service charge. Some banks have multiple options so go in person and explain you want the cheapest deal. Secondly, get one that has Saturday lobby hours. This is far more important than how many miles away it is. Thirdly, do they have on-line bill paying services and what do they cost.

10. How much will I need to open an account?

A.   At least $100.

11. Is it safe to keep all my money in one bank?

A. No need to worry about that. Deposits at most financial institutions are federally insured up to $100, 000.00. A famous western TV actor, Dale Robertson lost approximately $700,000 in a Savings and Loan collapse in Oklahoma a couple of decades ago. However, this is quite rare.

12. If I cannot afford to continue paying my car loan what can I do?

A.   Sell the car even if it is just for someone to take over payments. Or voluntarily turn it in. If you do the latter your credit will still be adversely affected. Another option is to cut your other expenses. Or you might be able to trade down with the same dealer or lender. Do not let the lender repossess without communicating with them first.

13. I am 17. How do I establish credit?

A.   When 18, you can start with a free FICO score
      and credit report. You do not have to pay anybody
      (Experian, Trans Union or Equifax) for a credit
      report.

14. How do you feel about transferring balances between
credit cards?

A.   Shakespeare wrote" Full of sound and fury, signifying
      nothing". Pay them off or reduce them. Transferring
      accomplishes nothing. Let us not confuse activity
      with progress.

15. I cannot pay my credit card bill. What will happen?

A.   Your life will be more difficult. Concentrate on paying
      current bills and not incurring any new debt.

16. Should I file a tax return even if I only work part-time
during the year?

A.   Yes. It is the only way to obtain a refund of part or all
      of what you paid in. And it is a good way to learn the
      tax code. And an even better way to qualify for debt
      if needed. Texas, Alaska, New Hampshire and Florida
      are a few states, which have no income taxes. If your
      state requires a state return, you will also need to file
      a federal return. For about $29 you can purchase an
      income tax program to do a simple return.

17. What is a 401k and how should I invest my money in
it?

It refers to Internal Revenue Code section 401-subsection
k. Invest in what you know. Everybody knows something. Stick

with the things you understand. If you know what makes the value go up and what makes it go down, it is a good choice for you. Be wary of trusting someone who earns a commission on your investment decision.

18. What about CD's?

    A.   If you have $10,000 or more that you do not need for three years, it is a good deal

19. Saving money is too hard. Can I just keep going month to month?

    A.   Not saving money is harder. You miss opportunities and live with more stress.

19. What is the best way to save for college?

Plan to live at home and start working at the earliest age possible. Save most of what you earn.

20. How much should I save for emergencies?

Whatever you have saved already, double it. If you have not yet started saving, plan for six months of your current net pay.

21. I read that the child tax credit is going to be $1,000 per child per year for several years. Is that true? Does that mean that my tax liability is reduced by that amount?

For calendar years 2005 through 2010, there will be a child tax credit of $1,000 per child per year. I make no predictions for the years beyond 2010. And yes it does mean that your tax due is reduced by that amount. That is the difference between a credit and a deduction. A credit is worth more since it is a dollar for dollar offset of taxes due and payable. A deduction on the other hand merely reduces the amount of money that the taxes are based upon.

For example, interest expense is of no taxable benefit if one utilizes the standard deduction, which most people do. If one itemizes deductions on Schedule A, then one merely reduces taxable income. Consider the case where a family has $12,000 in allowable interest on Schedule A and adjusted gross income of $80,000. This would mean that the taxes are calculated on $68,000 rather than $80,000. If a person were in a ten percent tax bracket, the $12,000 in interest only saved them $1,200 in taxes ($12,000 times ten percent).

The bottom line here is that the tax consequences can never be used to justify indebtedness.

22. I never know if my boyfriend and I should file as single, or married filing jointly or married filing separately or head of household. We could get married if it would help save on our taxes. Which way gets us the biggest refund?

If you are not married yet, I would not suggest that income taxes affect your decision. The tax consequences of the marital status are usually less than one percent of the total lost by each party in a divorce. Therefore, let us not confuse marriage with income tax strategy.

If you get married, it is usually better to file a joint return. One instance where a separate filing is advised is when one party has a high income and also high deductions. Also, if a married couple is already physically separated and contemplating divorce, a married filing separately status is well advised.

If one parent has children from a previous marriage, and they qualify as dependent children, it is often preferable for that parent to file as head of household.

The bottom line is that some credits and benefits are only available to couples filing jointly. One way to determine is to ask your tax preparer or software program to produce "what if" tax returns. Whichever way yields the biggest refund is probably the winner.